INDIAN & WESTERN EDUCATIONAL PHILOSOPHY

Prof. A.P. Sharma

UNICORN BOOKS

Publishers
UNICORN BOOKS
F-2/16, Ansari Road, Daryaganj, New Delhi-110002
☎ Ph.: 011-23275434, 23262683, 23250704
E-mail: info@unicornbooks.in • *Website:* www.unicornbooks.in

Branch : Mumbai
23-25, Zaoba Wadi, Thakurdwar, Mumbai-400002
☎ 022-22010941, 022-22053387
E-mail: unicornbooksmumbai@gmail.com

ISBN 978-81-7806-201-3

Edition: 2019

Printed at : Param Offsetters, Okhla, New Delhi-110020

Preface

A good number of books have already been written on Indian and Western Philosophies by eminent thinkers and philosophers like Dr. S. Radhakrishnan, M. Hirriyana, Das Gupta, J. N. Sinha, Brubacher, Edward J. Power and R. R. Rusk. Therefore, did I need to work upon such a book again? I think 'yes'. There was certainly a great need to write a book on philosophy that not only contained the principal ideas relating to Indian philosophical systems but to Western philosophical systems as well. It is because of that that this work is slightly different from that of the aforesaid great authors. I have strictly limited the discussions on the subjects keeping in view the interest of most of the graduate and post-graduate university students in the country. In view of the university requirement and students' need, the book is divided into two sections—Indian Philosophical systems and Western philosophical schools, including the educational implications relating to the problems of education belonging to both the systems.

My method of presenting the facts and the principal ideas relating to philosophy and education is very different from the works of most of the different authors in the sense that I have deliberately tried to avoid elaborate descriptions and discussions on many topics which I find don't have much place in the university syllabi. As such, unnecessary details regarding Indian and Western philosophical flights have been avoided as there is neither any basic need to keep them in one's memory nor any serious applicability of those issues in one's day-to-day life.

However, all important matters relating to the Indian or Western philosophy that have a bearing on human life and conduct have been taken into consideration. As such each philosophical system, whether orthodox or heterodox, has been dealt with utmost care in both the philosophical sections—Indian and Western. Care has also been taken to discuss each topic quite elaborately so that the reader can have a clearer view of each school of philosophy and be able to find answers to the difficult questions relating to education or the topics. I have tried honestly to present the material in such a lucid way that it may not only be helpful to the students of education to understand the basic concepts underlying each different systems clearly, but also be useful to them to discover answers to most of the difficult questions often asked at the university examinations at the degree or post-degree levels in the field of education. **Educational implications are either provided separately or are interwoven with each topic within different chapters, and are highlighted in bold**.

Although most of the material has been gathered from important texts and scholarly works, at several places objective analysis and critical reviews of the Indian and Western philosophical systems are reflected by me, to highlight certain important educational issues that are often not dealt with so intimately. Besides, the information relating to the Western and Indian philosophical systems is not only authentic but also highly informative. I have aimed to provide clear conceptions of various thorny philosophical problems that might often look difficult to the reader. Two important chapters in the text have also been added, one each in the areas of Indian and Western philosophical systems. These are---'Indian Philosophical Foundations' and 'What is Good?', with a view to providing the reader a better perspective about the main ideas commonly shared by all the schools of Indian Philosophy and to highlight the meaning of 'Good' which has always been a great concern of most Western thinkers. It is also a valuable precept in most countries of the world at all levels of schooling.

It has already been stated that the book is divided into two sections—Indian philosophical schools and Western philosophical systems. The second part that takes care of the Western philosophical ideology, deals with the meaning of philosophy and education, relation of philosophy with education and the scope of philosophy of education. This is followed by discussions on the elements of philosophy, philosophical schools and educational problems that have greatly influenced the realm of education. **In the third section (Western Philosophical Thought) of the book no material has been highlighted in bold as most of it deals with education directly.**

In both the sections of the book, within the chapters at different places, reflections are also made (*in italics*) on how the material given in the chapters is relevant to the modern educational system. Besides, at the end of each chapter questions have also been provided to show how the information implicit inside the chapters can be useful in tracing its relationship with education. Thus, the material presented in the chapters is expected to be not only highly relevant but also greatly informative to both, the teachers and the students of education at the post-graduate and graduate levels. My efforts will be greatly rewarded if the readers find this work useful in solving the problems relating to the domain of Indian and Western Educational Philosophy.

Author

25th December, 2009

The Good Curriculum

Naturalists and pragmatists emphasize the utility criterion of the good curriculum. They feel that the school's responsibility is to enable the child to [illegible] experience so that he can lead a worthwhile life. Their criterion is that the curriculum must include knowledge and skills that the child requires for future life. According to Aristotle children should be taught those useful things which are really necessary. They should be assisted to develop the habits, skills, interests and sentiments which they would need for their community. Dewey emphasizes that the child should always be considered as the centrepiece of a good curriculum. He stresses that to prepare the child for the future he must have a rich and full experience. His education should be based on his [illegible] abilities and interests.

[illegible] was to produce good soldiers. Physical [illegible] all that was important to the Spartans [illegible] aspect of education particularly [illegible] was also in evidence [illegible]

[illegible] the importance of physical [illegible] child so that he could become a [illegible] that a healthy mind is found in [illegible] for both physical and mental [illegible] curriculum.

Contents

Naturalism and Education

(i) No Institutional Education

According to John Adams, naturalism is a term which is loosely applied to systems of training which are not dependent upon schools and books. Naturalistic educators prefer to start from the actual life of pupils and to utilize this in bringing pupils back to nature. All training and education must be in keeping with the natural development of the child.

Rousseau, for instance, was appalled by the formal schooling practices of his time. Education for the pupil Emile was to proceed according to nature. "Our foolish and pedantic methods," he wrote, "are always preventing children from learning what they could learn much better by themselves." Emile was, therefore, to be taken away from his parents, away from society and school and to be educated by an ideal tutor in close and direct contact with nature. The child's whole environment is the book from which he unconsciously enriches his memory.

(ii) [illegible]

Rousseau's educational [illegible] lasting [illegible] on education [illegible] central [illegible]

SECTION A

PART - I

Indian Philosophical Schools

Chapter One

Indian Philosophical Foundations

Before trying to understand the meaning of philosophy, it is imperative that one must also know the meaning of the term *darshan*. Though not quite identical in meaning, yet the term *darshan* can be equated to philosophy in the Indian sense. The word *darshan* is derived from the Sanskrit root *drs* which means to see. When *lyut* is added to it, it leads to mean 'through the instrumentality of which something is to be observed or seen'. This kind of function of observing or seeing can be done both by the external and internal eyes. The internal eye is also taken to be as divine eyes, wisdom or vision of knowledge. Thus, the term *darshan* is used both in the abstract and concrete form. In actual practice this term consists of a body of arguments for and against the existence of certain opposite or contradictory elements like 'whether *atman* is pure, real and existent; whether God exists; whether 'good' can be attained; whether heaven or hell exists or whether the Ultimate Truth (Being) can be realized?' In the inquiry about the reality lies the culmination of all the Indian philosophy. But every system of Indian thought has tried to discover how to attain the Ultimate Truth and therefore, it is considered as the *summum bonum* of religion, ethics and metaphysics as well.

When we try to trace the roots of Indian philosophical system we look for that in the *Vedas* which can be broadly divided into two sections. One is related to knowledge (*jnana kanda*) and the other deals with rituals (*karma kanda*). The *Brahmana* scriptures deal about the *karma kanda,* and the *Upanishads* and the *Aranyakas* deal with knowledge (*jnana kanda*). As there is a great store of knowledge in the *Vedas,* it has resulted in winning great respect from both, the Indians as well as the outsiders who have tried to understand the right meanings of the *sutras* contained in the *Vedas*. Broadly, the Indian philosophical systems have been divided into two classes, viz. atheistic (*nastik*) and theistic (*astic*), or non-believers and believers respectively. Though these two terms—*nastic* and *astik* signify a non-believer and a believer in God's existence, it does not mean that one, who does not believe in God, also does not believe in rebirth. Both the Buddhists and Jains, though do not believe in God's existence, but believe in transmigration in some way.

The Believers (*Astikas*)

All the schools of Indian philosophy that believe in the testimony of the *Vedas* are known as the *astikas*. These are six in number and are known as *Sad Darshan*. These are: Mimansa, Vedanta, Samkhya, Yoga, Nyaya and Vaisesika. Out of these six schools of Mimansa is the only system which does not believe in God's existence. Therefore, the meaning of *astika* is limited to 'as a believer in the authority of the *Vedas* only. The *astika* class of thought is divided into two types—one class is directly based upon the *Vedic* scriptures. These include the Mimamsa and Vedanta systems. Of these two, Mimamsa emphasizes upon the ritualistic aspect of the *Vedas* and the second, *Vedanta*, upon the knowledge aspect. The other class belongs to the schools that are not directly based on the *Vedic* scriptures but accept the testimony of the *Vedas* and stay in harmony with them as far as their own view points are concerned. These schools are Samkhya, Yoga, Nyaya and Vaisesika

The Non-believers (*Nastiks*)

The non-believers or *nastik* class of Indian philosophical systems are the Carvakas, the Jains, and the Buddha schools of thought as they hold no belief in the *Vedas'* testimony. These schools originated as a reaction against the *Vedic* system and tradition. The Carvaka system has openly defied the *Vedic* traditions and states that they are full of repetitions and contain lies created by the cunning priests to misguide simple people. This sort of prejudicial criticism against the *Vedas* has been widely criticized by the scholars and thinkers like Udayana and Vainkathnath. The Jains also don't believe in the authority of the *Vedas* as they believe in the word of their Tirthankaras. The Buddhists also condemn blind faith in the *Vedas*. Still the both, the Jains and the Buddhists have not displayed the utter disrespect for the *Vedas* that Carvakas have done.

Universal Characteristics of Indian Philosophical Schools

The realization of eternal truth has always been in the background of time and culture of a particular country but the desire of attainment of the eternal truth transcends the barriers of time and place. Therefore, the philosophical systems of different countries, including Indian, are also deeply influenced by their own culture. Despite the diversity (already reported) contained in the Indian philosophical systems, there are certain common characteristics that are characterized by some kind of fundamental unity. In view of that we present the following common features of the Indian philosophical systems.

The Common Features

1. The Reality of the Spirit

Indian Philosophy is spiritual in nature and holds belief in the reality of the soul and seeks to realize it in its true form. The soul's realization has been the common goal of all the schools of Indian philosophy except the Carvakas. From Upanishads to Samkhya, Yoga, Nyaya, Vaisesika and Vedanta have been inspired alike by the same thought.

2. Proximity to Life

All schools of Indian philosophy are close to life, therefore, they don't simply try to seek fulfilment of intellectual desires, but also keep higher aims in view. The founders of these schools wanted to tackle the ultimate problems of life, which are bred in life itself. The Indian classics viz. *the Gita* and the *Upanishads*, have never been separated from human life and project the ideals and feelings of the Indian masses.

3. Spiritual Discontentment

In fact, Indian philosophers were never satisfied with simply ordinary philosophical pursuits. Thus, Indian philosophy originates with the discontent of the spirit with man's temporal life. As a consequence it aims at a divine change in one's life. But this sort of spiritual discontentment is not pessimistic. Take for example of Buddha's pursuits of truth and his efforts to discover a solution to human misery. Though Buddha emphasized the unpleasant side of the world, yet he also suggested the Eightfold Path which if pursued earnestly, could help end all worldly travails. In this manner Indian philosophy though originating in pessimism, moves forward to attain happiness and salvation finally.

4. Ultimate Goal is Liberation

Indian philosophy aims at the divine transformation of life and redemption from worldly miseries. Except *Carvakas*, all the schools of philosophy whether *astika* or *nastika*, though differing in their views on liberation, hold that liberation means freedom from the bondage of ignorance which helps man to be free from all misery and the ills of flesh. The final stage of liberation is total freedom which transcends ethics and religion as well. The right kind of education also aims at such kind of liberation as its primary aim is to liberate human beings from ignorance which is the main source of misery in life.

5. Ignorance

All the Indian philosophers reckon that the root cause of human bondage is ignorance. This ignorance could be intellectual, spiritual and psychological as well. The four great truths suggested by Buddha and what Samkara suggested in *Vedanta* can help humans to get redeemed from the ignorance and help reach freedom or liberation. Hence, it is imperative to get rid of ignorance if one wants to be free from the fetters of bondage

6. Practising Yoga to Attain *Moksha*

Most schools of Indian philosophy suggest that practice of yoga is necessary to get freedom from psychological and spiritual ignorance. The eightfold yoga of Patanjali has been accepted in some degrees by almost all schools of philosophy. The practice of Yama, Niyama, Asana, Samadhi and Nididhyaṣana, etc is considered as a way to dispel ignorance. The transformation of life through knowledge is the aim of spiritual practice or *Sadhana*. Most Indian philosophical systems give equal emphasis on both, knowledge (*jnana*) and spiritual practice (*Sadhana*). This practice has both sides—negative (if done incorrectly) and positive (if done correctly).

7. Psychology as the Basis

Most Indian philosophers have tried to explain psychological facts related to human life minutely. **Starting from Buddha to Patanjali including Samkara and Ramanujam, all have tried to explain how human mind or psychology is related to one's happiness and sorrow. Most yogic exercises are held to cure physical and mental maladies and to attaining mental concentration which can help restoring long-term happiness. The philosophy of Vedanta gives a minute analysis of the different stages of human consciousness such as *Jagrti*, *Svapna*, *Susupti* and *Turiya*. Based on the experience of life, most schools of Indian philosophy go deeper to seek the way to human freedom and salvation. All such ideas are deeply related to the realm of education.**

8. Fusion of Philosophy and Religion

The most outstandingly common feature of the Indian philosophical system is not to seek religion and philosophical problems rigidly. The idea or concept of Dharma has been used in a wide and comprehensive sense. The truth is that transformation of life and release from worldly misery constitute the common goal of philosophy as well as of religion. Most schools of Indian philosophy, except *Carvakas*, discover that the identification of problems in relation to man and God is very common. Besides they also consider that intellectual and spiritual experiences are the decisive factors to ascertain the soundness of religious standards. The meaning of 'being awake' in Buddhist thought or

philosophy is related to mental maturity or heightened mental awareness, which is at par with nirvana, salvation or *moksha*. In fact, providing mental maturity through the right kind of experiences at school and at the other levels of education is one the important aspects of education. Therefore, this aspect of Indian Philosophy is deeply related to education.

9. Intellectualism

Most Indian philosophical systems seek the truth in their own independent way and approach human problems with an open mind devoid of any prejudices. Following this sort of procedure they try to solve the problems through strong and sound arguments, propound their own thesis and reject other schools logically. They hold that to reach the truth, open philosophical discussions (*Sastrartha*) must be held and results should be reached through logical pursuits only. This is how logic got a free play in Indian philosophy and through it the sages and the philosophers created a congenial environment for its full and free development through intellectual procedures only.

10. Universal Welfare

While pursuing truth through intellectual means, Indian philosophers always laid emphasis on universal welfare rather than looking at any single aspect of human life. Samkara, Buddha and Mahavir were not only eminent thinkers but also renowned social reformers. The Indian philosophical system did not aim only at individual salvation but also aimed at the spiritual transformation of society. In this respect we have the best examples of Buddha and Mahavir, who even after getting enlightenment, stayed for a long time to help people get redeemed. The *Gita* also aims at human salvation and universal welfare which has always been the aim of right education throughout.

11. Implicit With Vitality

In nature and pursuit the Indian philosophical systems are totally dynamic. When one philosophical system became very popular, some other systems developed and counteracted against the prevailing system, providing logical arguments to seek the truth in its own way. Through the diversity of Materialism (of Carvakas), Spiritualism, Dualism, Non-dualism and Qualified Monism, etc., one can visualize the unbroken chain of intellectual action and reaction leading to provide the dynamism projected in the Indian philosophical systems.

12. Faith in the Ancient Wisdom

Most Indian philosophical systems have a common faith in the Vedas, the *Bhagwad Gita* and the *Upanishads*. All the *astika* philosophical systems hold the scriptures as testimony, though this testimony is not based on words but on intuitive truth. As a matter of fact the *Vedas* are the repositories of the intuitive knowledge of the learned Indian seers. Such a faith in the ancient wisdom accounts for a particular order. This order is mostly found in all the Indian philosophical systems and cannot be taken as a blind faith. A great philosopher like Samkara, who considers himself merely a commentator, likes to use logic when faced with any contradictions. Thus, a continued faith in the past and the scriptures is not a blind faith but is often backed by logic.

13. Faith in Universal Moral Order

Faith in *Rta* or universal moral order is another important common aspect of the Indian philosophers. Such a universal system is termed as *'Rta'* in the *Vedas*, *'Apurva'* in Mimamsa and *'Adrsta'* in Nyaya-Vaisesika. According to it all living beings, gods, plants and the entire universe move in accordance with one universal moral pattern or principle. In the Western world, idealists like Socrates, Plato and Aristotle also held the same belief that everything in the universe is moving in the direction to attain perfection.

14. Faith in Karma

Almost all the Indian schools of philosophy believe in the theory of *Karma*. According to it, the results of our actions (*karmaphala*) are always with us in the form of impressions (*samskaras*) and they affect and direct the course of our lives. In this manner the world is just like a stage, where every one of us is preordained to perform one's part according to one's *karma*. To be free from the bondage of *karma* one needs liberation. Different systems of Indian philosophy have suggested different methods and ways to attain liberation and to be free from the yoke of *karma*.

15. Belief in Rebirth

Almost all the schools of Indian philosophy hold the belief that rebirth takes place in view of one's *karma* done in the past life. Thus, the theory of *karma* and belief in rebirth go hand in hand. On account of the bondage created by our longings we act in our life, which in turn forms our *karma*. One can be free from this sort of bondage of rebirth by following a particular way or method, as suggested by Buddha or some of the *Vedic* sagas. Except Carvakas most schools of Indian philosophy believe that there is certainly a way that can help one to get redeemed and get freedom from rebirth. They call it total liberation.

Accusations Against Indian Philosophy

Some Western philosophers have levelled charges against Indian philosophy trying to undermine its magnanimity though most ideas, propounded by the Indian philosophical seers thousands of years back, are still very popular with the masses. Some of these charges are listed below:

1. Dominating Pessimism

Some Western thinkers reckon that Indian philosophy consists of profound pessimism and in it there is less scope of optimism which is the very basis of human hope and happiness. But such Western thinkers are unaware of the real nature and profound undertones that go on continually in the Indian philosophy. It is pessimistic in the sense that it originates in dissatisfaction with the present conditions of materialistic world. The world is full of hardships and implicit with frustration when material goals are not achieved. Indian philosophers wisely analyse this wretched plight of the world and proceed to achieve higher goals in life to achieve lasting happiness. Therefore, that kind of pessimism is indispensable for the progress in life. It helps us think for better goals and inspires to put more efforts to reach the right goal in life.

The truth is that Indian philosophy is wholly optimistic about the ultimate goal of life. Most philosophical systems in India aim at liberation, which is not an escape from or an end of life, but just transformation of life. It helps man to transcend from the delusions of the world and to attain everlasting bliss after realizing the true self. Dr S. Radhakrishnan (Ind.Phil.vol.I,p5) rightly comments on it. 'Indian thinkers are pessimistic in so far as they look upon the world order as an evil and a lie, but they are optimistic since they feel that there is a way out of it into the realm of truth which is also goodness.'

2. Too Much Reverence for Tradition

Since scriptures are regarded as an authoritative source of knowledge, the Western thinkers have labelled it dogmatism. The

Vedas, the *Upanishads* and the *Gita* have always been quoted by the Indian philosophers as a great source of knowledge. This has led Western thinkers (perhaps due to their ignorance) to lay the charge of dogmatism against the Indian philosophical way of thinking. Indian philosophy, in fact, has grown out of logical discussions, constantly evaluating, criticizing and reevaluating the principles of life that would promise a delusion free life. Faith in the *Vedas* must not be misconceived as dogmatism. On the contrary they enshrine the intuitive experiences of our intellectual seers. That experience can be shared by every person provided he/she tries to get it dispassionately. Faced with contradictions during these experiences, Indian philosophers have sought the help of intellect and logic and developed profound philosophical principles. Celebrated logicians like Samkara, Ramanujam, Madhava, and Nimbarka etc., have propounded profound philosophical theories in the light of their own personal experiences. In view of that one must admit that though Indian philosophy does believe in its tradition, but is not based on blind faith. It is based on true experience evolved through logical canons and critical inquiry.

3. Not Ethical but Spiritual Only

Some Western thinkers hold that there is practically no projection of ethical thinking within Hindu way of philosophizing and in its place spirituality has been considered superior to ethics. If we think objectively we find that spirituality is always superior to ethical barriers as freedom or liberation is beyond the boundaries of the good and bad. A liberated person certainly transcends the ethical realm. Therefore, it is evident that the Indian philosophy aimed at a much higher level than limiting itself to the fields of ethics. But ethics is also not overlooked. A person, who has attained liberation or perfection in the spiritual field, definitely rises above moral conflicts because he is beyond any sinful activities. Besides, one cannot deny that before the attainment of the spiritual stage, ethical considerations are necessary for every human being. Almost every school of Indian philosophy has considered it thoughtfully except Carvakas. Jaina, Buddha, Vedanta and Samkhya have taken into consideration different ethical precepts in details giving them a proper place prior to the attainment of liberation.

4. Indian Philosophy is Unprogressive

Some Western thinkers also charge Indian philosophy with being unprogressive and bogged down in old ruts. Most of its material is based on facts that have been borrowed down mainly from the *Upanishads* and the *Gita*. But such charges are totally unfounded as philosophy deals with eternal things comprehended by intuition. Such truth(s) never change with scientific discoveries or progress. One must also accept that the *Gita* and the *Upanishads* are as good and inspiring even today as they were in the past. Besides, the *Upanishads* and the *Gita* have been interpreted by different philosophers like, Samkara, Ramanujam, Sri Aurobindo and Vinoba Bhave in their own way. It makes Indian philosophy progressive as with the change of time philosophical truths have been rediscovered in new ways though basic meanings have not been changed. Besides, the Jaina, Buddha, Nyaya, Vaisesika, Samkhya, Yoga and Vedanta, which are different schools of philosophy, have not only presented their own theories but also refuted the theories of their opponents. All this is a testimony that reflects that Indian philosophy is essentially progressive.

Practical Attempt to Attain the Truth

Indian philosophy began out of curiosity. The seers who created the *Vedas* wondered at nature's phenomena. 'Why all that had been happening since long?' was the basic query they made to understand nature and tried to seek answers to the causes of things. For example, 'Why all the rivers flow towards the sea and why the sea is never brimming over?' Thus, the seers looked at nature with awe and tried to know the reality behind all those things that made them wonder. Thus, basically, Indian philosophy has always been a practical attempt to realize the truth. Besides, the aim of the realization has never been just to satisfy intellectual desire, but 'how to find a way for a better life, which would be higher as well as more happiness giving. The flight of imagination contained in the *Vedas*, was replaced in the *Upanishads*. **The *Upanishadic* seers aimed at not simply knowing but also on being or becoming. Consequently they prayed very aptly, 'Lead me to truth. Keep me away from falsehood. Deliver me from darkness to light, from death to immortality.' All this can never be out of the realm of education as it too aims to deliver humans from ignorance (darkness) to light (enlightenment).**

As the *Upanishads* are the sources of almost all the Indian philosophical systems, every school of Indian philosophy emphasized on the realization of truth and on the knowledge about it. For example, Buddha altogether rejected discussing the issues like 'whether soul exists or rebirth takes place or heaven or hell are there', and emphasized on practising the 'eight-fold path which he considered a way to get redeemed. In this way it is not metaphysics but ethics which is the keynote in Buddhism. Jains also prescribe the way to renunciation from the right *Karma*. Three Jewels or 'Tri Ratna' i.e. right realization (*samyak darsan*), right knowledge (*samyak jnana*) and right character (*samyak caritra*)' are Jainas' key precepts to attain *Nirvana.* Right character includes another five precepts which are: Non-violence (*ahimsa*), truth (*satya*), non-stealing (*ssteya*), celibacy (*brahmcarya*), and non-covetousness (*aparigraha*).

The *summum bonum* or the highest aim of life in view of all the six traditional schools of Indian philosophy is to attain liberation. Yoga is the practical aspect of Samkhya philosophy. The eight-fold path prescribed by yoga is an unparalleled contribution to attain liberation through spiritual practice and leads to attain a unique human energy by which yogis (seers) can perform impossible tasks. Its proper practice can help cessation of varied impulses of mind and makes it totally calm and free of any delusion. Indian yogis from Patnjali to Aurobindo, Yogananda, Vivekananda, and Jiddu Krishnamurti have constantly tried to improve and practise this method of yoga to cultivate such energies in man to transform into the realm of divine. Even Samkara, a great logician, prescribed a four-fold path as an introduction for the study of *Vedanta.* These four-fold procedures consist of the following:

(1) Understanding the distinction between the perishable and eternal

(2) Abandoning the desire for possessing all mundane and super-mundane pleasures.

(3) Attaining of six means of Sama, Dama, Sraddha, Samadhana, Uparati and Titiksa.

(4) Possessing a living desire to attain liberation.

Even after acquiring the above indicated four-fold path, Samkara prescribes listening to scriptures, meditation, and concentration as essentials to achieve liberation. Therefore, like other Indian schools,

Advaita Vedanta also emphasized greatly to practise the ways leading to human liberation. Besides Samkara, another scholar, Ramanujam, a great devote of God, reflected that devotion was the life blood of all philosophy. He also presented a practical way to attain liberation and stated that 'Devotion implies surrender (*prapatti*), which is implicit with the following six things. These are:

(1) One's thought, action and will should be in tune with God.

(2) It must be kept in mind that if thought is not in line with God's devotion, both action and will go against God.

(3) One must keep full 'faith in God' which always has divine protection.

(4) One should keep in mind that 'continuous praying' should be done to seek divine protection.

(5) One must surrender completely to God.

(6) One should feel all the time that one is totally dependent on God.

Educationally Invaluable

Both the approaches of Samkara and Ramanujam elaborately describe the practical aspects of spiritual quest. Therefore, Indian philosophical systems synthesize theory with practice and thought with action, and seek to help human beings to lead a happier and integrated life with which endless bliss could be attained in life.

In view of that our modern education system needs to be more practical to help the students not only to learn the subject matter theoretically, but practice most of their aspects too in their day-to-day lives. For example, knowledge of geography, history, biological sciences or mathematics, could be certainly helpful

to them in many ways in their daily lives. Besides, our Vedas, Upanishads, ancient scriptures and reflections made by the seers like Samkara and Ramanujam, Vivekananda and others are highly relevant as far as students' character development is concerned. What we need today is to foster good conduct among our students by making them remember and practise the moral and social precepts that the Vedic and Upanishadic seers identified. If our educators can bring some of those value-ridden ideas within the framework of educational curriculum at different levels of schooling in some way, it would not only be a great service to education but will also be a tremendous help to our students to learn those values which are surely prerequisite to lead a happy and successful life in future.

Questions

(1) Describe briefly the common characteristics of Indian philosophy and trace their relevance to education.

(2) What are the common accusations against Indian philosophy? How far do you agree with them?

(3) To what extent have the Indian Philosophical systems truly attempted to help realize the truth in one's life? What is its relevance to education?

(4) How far Samkara's and Ramanujam's philosophical approaches are relevant to our modern educational system? Discuss critically.

Chapter Two

The Philosophy Contained in the Vedas

Historical Interpretations

Traditionally it is accepted that there are **four *Vedas***—the Rg Veda, the Sam Veda, the Yajur Veda, and the Atharva Veda. Regardless of this division, the Vedas are all a single comprehensive account of knowledge. The division is simply made on the basis of the subject and the hymns provided in each section. For example, the *mantras* (sacred chanting) contained in the Yajur Veda are chanted at the occasion of offering sacrifices during *Yajna* (fire lit for the offering), the hymns of Rg Veda are simply uttered and the hymns in Sam Veda are sung. The hymns contained in the Atharv Veda relate to the knowledge of natural objects. The subject matter of these four *Vedas* is broadly divided into two parts—the *Jnana Kanda* and the *Karma Kanda*. The first implying the theoretical aspect and the other concerned with the practical and actual conduct. The former provides knowledge about spiritual meditation while the latter explains the forms of the prayer and sacrifice.

The *Vedas* hold that the entire creation is caused by an omnipotent and omniscient power. In addition, they also discuss in detail the subjects related to moral conduct, virtue, sin and theory of *Karma*. They strongly hold that the pains of the flesh (body) can be removed by worship. Most historians believe that Rg Veda came into existence around 2000 B.C. It contains references to the *varna* (caste) and the *asrama* systems, which are taken to be the fundamental elements in the social organization of the Aryans. Today it is difficult to determine how much has been added to this aspect of the Vedas later on.

The *Vedas* are not merely philosophical discourse unfolding the nature of spirituality, they also discuss all possible topics, spiritual and mundane (earthly). As action is required to attain the objectives, therefore the *Karma Kanda* is a great necessity. In the view of a Western scholar named Wilson, Indian philosophy originated initially from the dissatisfaction with earthly life. The prime aim of Indian philosophy therefore, has been to find ways to get rid of suffering and sorrow caused by ignorance.

The *Vedic* seers, based on their intuitive knowledge, have expressed their divine vision of the Ultimate Reality which is not the reflection of their individuality. That means that the Ultimate Reality had manifested Himself in the form of *Vedic* hymns and the seers were simply the media chosen by the Ultimate Being for that purpose. It unfolds the attitude of the Indian (*Astika*) seers and philosophers, who considered the *Vedas* to possess the ultimate and eternal truth and authority. These truths have been preserved through a ceaseless tradition maintained by the teacher and the pupil from ancient times. Thus, they are also known as *Sruti*.

Though there are four *Vedas*, they are one and eternal. Each *Veda* contains three parts viz. *Mantra, Brahmana,* and *Upanishads*. The collection of hymns is known as *Samhitas*; the *Brahmanas* deal with *Karma Kanda* and philosophical thought is contained in the *Upanishads* and *Aranyakas*. The *Aranyakas* fall between *Brahmanas* and the *Upanishads*. It is only the *Atharva Veda* which is different from the other *Vedas* as it contains mostly historical narration in it.

Interpretations Contained in the Hymns

Divergent views have been expressed by thinkers as regards the interpretations of the *Vedic* hymns. Some of the very important of such ideas are presented hereunder for the benefit of the reader:

1. Invocation to the Natural Powers

Most *Vedic* hymns are rich in terms of containing prayers to gods, who are the personification of the natural powers. The religion referred to in the *Vedas* directs us to worship nature. Thus a great number of the hymns are simple and naive, and implicit with religious consciousness of a mind which is almost free from the complexity that was introduced in it later years.

2. Ritualistic Explanation

Some western scholars contain that in the *Vedic* hymns there is great description of the methods of sacrifice. The *Rg-Veda* is primarily the work of a primitive people who laid great emphasis on ritualism. The gods and goddesses identified in the *Vedas* represent different articles needed for the *Yagna* so they are not profound and much meaningful.

3. Allegorical Representations

Many western authors reckon that all the hymns in the *Vedas* are full of allegory as the gods and goddesses of the *Vedic* times are symbolic to social customs and represent the prevalent conventions only.

4. Monotheistic Explanations

The hymns in the *Rg-Veda* contain explanations that almost clearly depict a monotheistic interpretation of gods and goddesses. In several hymns there is a reference of someone like *Devadhideva*, which simply means God of gods. Both Roth and Swami Dayananda hold the same view about the interpretation of a supreme God referred to in the hymns. Thus, though there is a reference of many semi-Gods in the *Vedas*, the supreme God is only one.

5. Implicit with Mysticism

Seers like Sri Aurobindo find that the *Vedic* hymns are full of mystic philosophy and the Gods and Goddesses are symbols of psychological processes. For example, the sun symbolizes intellect while fire and moon represent 'determination and feeling' respectively. Sri Aurobindo reflects that the *Rg-Veda* itself is one of the considerable documents of knowledge that remains with us from the early period of human thought containing spiritual and psychological knowledge of the race concealed in the form of allegory for reasons now very difficult to determine. He contended that 'one of the leading principles of presenting human knowledge under the veil of mystery was perhaps the sacredness, secrecy of self-knowledge and the true knowledge about God.

All these mystical ideas regarding *Vedas* often appear to be contradictory on the surface but they visualize the same truth from different angles. As different hymns were created by different seers, so they appear different in their meaning and import. Therefore, none of the interpretations regarding the *Vedic* hymns may be regarded as absolutely correct. The *Vedas* do not deal with only one exclusive subject. There is philosophy and religion on one hand, and science and magic on the other hand. Naturally because of that all the hymns cannot be interpreted in a uniform manner.

6. The Ultimate Aims

The seers were fully alive to the miseries of earthly existence and longed to attain freedom from worldly ills. Therefore, they always tried to find the way to attain perfect bliss along with the way to perfect knowledge. From this point of view Vedantic Education is highly relevant to a student of education or to all those who choose teaching as their vocation. In view of that these two important aspects of human life were the only goals for them in human life. As the *Vedic* seers were anxious to conquer death they prayed for longevity in the *Vedas*. They knew the different ways to invoke gods and deities. They had full faith in the effectiveness of prayers so they prayed for attaining knowledge and perfect happiness. As they were desirous to attain ultimate knowledge, they subdued every sort of egotism and surrendered themselves to God. They had full faith that communion between the human soul and God could lead one to the right knowledge and happiness. Hence, the *Vedas* contend that realization of the ***Abhaya Jyoti*** was the only procedure to attain emancipation from the human ills. Consequently, they prayed to God: *"O Aditya: By your grace and kindness I can realize the Abhaya Jyoti.*

In the Vedas different sorts of prayers are suggested for different types of people in accordance to their duties and social obligations. Common men are not entitled for every form of prayers and worship. The seers held that good deeds and pure conduct was as much necessary as knowledge. Thus, penitence, prayers, simple diet, serenity in thought and purity in heart were essential for the realization of the Ultimate Being. Greed, hypocrisy, pride, anger and heartlessness are unwanted and must be eradicated resolutely. Only those who followed the righteous path, were truthful, meritorious and also followed the right action had the right to attain the realization of the Ultimate Being. **All such thoughts are highly relevant to the domain of education as they lay stress on the formation of right habits and right actions among students, leading them to cultivate right conduct which is one of the aims of education at all times.**

7. The Theory of Karma

The *Vedas* advocate the theory of *Karma*. Descriptions like 'Protector of good deeds' or 'Seer of good and evil actions' or 'Master of all Karma' have often been used for the Gods in the *Vedas*. Many hymns show that good actions lead to immortality and human soul undergoes many a cycle of birth and death according to its deeds. The *Vedas* reflect that man suffers in this life on account of the results of actions done in his previous life. The *Vedas* hold that evil tendencies of the present life are due to the evil actions committed in the previous life. Some *Vedic* hymns contain the seers' praying to God to condone the misdeeds of a previous life. They also refer to the accumulated and destined *Karma*. The hymns also reflect that the people who do good deeds go to *Brahmaloka* via *Devayana*. But those who indulge in ordinary deeds go to the *Chandraloka* via *Pitryana*. **The idea of cultivation of good Karma is certainly a prerequisite to lead a good and contented life in future. Therefore, all our efforts in the field of education should be directed to help our students to fostering social values among them by introducing various sorts of curricular activities like participating in regular games, outdoor activities and by organizing social service camps through which they may conceive the problems of the community and help people in eradicating some of their ills.**

8. The Vedic Religion

Most of the hymns in the Rg-Veda extol the gods who are considered the masters of the moving spirits of the different powers of nature. They are not separated in watertight compartments like the Greek gods. Not only do they represent the natural powers they are also co-related with one another and don't possess any crystallized individuality. The large number of gods indicated in the *Vedas* provided us an idea that they are polytheistic. But there are hymns that give the idea that these gods are monotheistic. Both these views are not totally acceptable. The fact is that the *Vedic* hymns are not identical in their approach and content. They are also not the products of any specific seers of a specific period. One can see a kind of gradual evolution in *Vedic* ideology. In fact, both monotheistic and polytheistic propensities run side by side in the *Vedas*. Living with nature the seers identified its powers, which overawed them. The specific power of nature which impressed them most was referred to as Parama Deva or the highest God by the seers.

In this respect Prof Max Muller states: "A belief in single gods, each in turn standing out as the highest. Since the gods are thought of specially ruling in their own areas, the singers (seers) in their special concerns and desires, call most of all on that god to whom they ascribe the most power in the matter, to whose department, if I may say so, their wish belongs........" (The Rg Veda, p. 23) Thus, in the view of many scholars, the *Vedas* begin with polytheism, and progress through henotheism to monotheism, which are three different stages of evolutionary history of the *Vedic* gods and religion as well. But the Vedic philosophy does not culminate at monotheism. It concludes in ***monism***. There are quite a number of hymns that clearly indicate the seers' mood and invocation to only one Ultimate God. For example,

1. All the gods are but the organs of the body of the soul of the universe. Nirukta, (7.4.9)
2. All that was, that is and that will be is but the *purusa.* (Rg-Veda, 10.90.)
3. The true essence of the gods is only one. (*Vedic Mythology, pp.*16-17)
4. Though pervading the whole universe, He transcends it all. (Rg-Veda, 10.90.3)

9. Origin of the Universe

There are different views contained in the *Vedas* about the origin of the universe. It is thought to have originated with *Agni* or fire. After that heaven, earth, day, night, water and other things came into being. Every soul came out of *Trasta.* It is also believed that Indra created the earth and heaven and the three worlds as well as the living beings. Later on the seers held that Viswa Karma and Varuna created the universe. This indicates clearly that the *Vedic* seers attributed any gods as the creators of something in view of their wishes, but it must be kept in view that the *Vedas* did not consider the various gods as separate entities. In the Rg Veda it is clearly mentioned that Sat, Antarikasa and Vyoma existed prior to the existence of the universe. There was darkness everywhere and none existed except one. There was water, but no light. That One originated from Tamas, which was a latent consciousness prior to the creation of the universe. It was after that that the wonders of the universe came into existence out of it.

Tamas is an omnipresent power and is the fountain head of all the three processes—knowledge, desire and action. Likewise the *purusa* hymn in the Yajur Veda indicates one omnipresent power as the originator of the universe. This all-pervading power has been described variously as Viswa Karma, the Unique, the Omnipresent, Paramavyoman, Paramapad and the Ultimate Being.

10. The Underlying Principle of the Cosmos

The principle underlying the cosmic evolution is termed as **Rta** by *Vedic* seers. Rta could simply mean the course of things and it roughly corresponds to that of *Karma* in human life. Perhaps by observing the orderly movements of the sun, the moon, the stars, the day and the night as well as the seasons would have given that sort of idea in the minds of the seers. The external universe is just its manifestation. Universe is changeable but Rta is not changeable and is eternal. In the beginning the meaning of Rta was limited to the course of the sun, the moon, the stars and the seasons etc, but gradually as the seers put more thought to it, they found it all pervading. So the initial meaning was changed. Instead of keeping its course fixed to the movements of the sun, the moon and the stars etc., its connotation became more comprehensive. It was gradually taken to signify the ethical course of gods and men. They thought that the entire universe depended on Rta and moved with it. Then the seers started considering that the creation of the universe was not just accidental, it was created with a more profound purpose and order was implicit in it.

11. Identity of Atman and Brahman

The belief in the identity of Atman and Brahman expressed so often even today by all those who hold the belief in the Sanatan Dharma, can be traced back to the hymns of the *Vedas*. It was further developed in the *Upanishads* and then it became one of the cardinal principles of Indian philosophy. Thus, the hymns of the Vedic period are much more than the scriptures of old but one finds in them important thought currents implicit in the later Indian philosophy. The *Jnana* and *Karma Kandas* were completely developed by the *Upanishads* and by the *Brahmans* respectively. Even the *Bhagvada Gita* drives its inspiration from the ideas contained in the *Upanishads* and *the Brhmans.* In Vedic thought one finds a combination of knowledge and religion and it contains the first reaction of humans towards the phenomenon of nature. In that respect the philosophy contained in the *Vedas* is certainly a source of all Indian philosophy.

Questions

1. What kind of divergent views have been expressed by the thinkers in relations to the interpretations of the *Vedic* hymns? Discuss them briefly indicating their relationship to education if any?
2. What short of religious views have been installed in the Vedic hymns? Has there been any departure in the way of Indian thinking as far as gods' conception is concerned since the time the Vedas were created? Does it have any bearing on the realm of education in your opinion?
3. What could have caused seers to consider that truth was monistic and not monotheistic? Does it affect the ways of thinking and living in our country in any way?
4. What is the ultimate goal of life according to the Vedic seers? How did they intend to attain that in life? In what respect is the ultimate goal of life proposed by the Vedic seers related to education?

5. What does Rta signifies in Indian philosophical thought? How did the ideas contained in Rta at the initial stage change gradually? Why did they change and what was the impact of this change on the Indian way of thinking? In what way are these ideas important in the field of education?
6. In what manner is the theory of *Karma* propounded by *Vedic* seers helpful to foster good conduct in our students? Discuss with examples.

Chapter Three

Philosophy Implicit in the Upanishads

Historical Perspective

For want of evidence it is difficult to decide exactly when the *Upanishads* were created. However, the traditional viewpoint is that the *Upanishads*, like the *Samhitas, the Brahmans* and *the Aranyakas* also form part of the *Vedas.* Keeping in view the testimony of the Buddhist scriptures, it can be inferred that some *Upanishads* were created before the time of Buddha, who was born in the sixth century B.C. Thus, some *Upanishads* were composed before 600 B.C. The distinguished among them are the *Chandogya, the Brhadaranyaka, the Kena, the Aitereya* and *the Katha* etc. The *Bhagwad Gita* is also considered as the essence of the *Upanishads and* is a part of the *Mahabharata.* Therefore, some *Upanishads* must have been written before *Mahabharat*, which took place before 3000 B.C. In this way it is presumed that the *Upanishads* were composed between 600 to 3000 B.C. (R.N.S, p 28). For thousands of years the *Upanishads* were preserved through teacher and taught tradition in the form of *Srti* and their writing must have started before 600 B.C.

Various *Upanishads* are attached to different *Vedas* and are classified according to their relationship with the *Rg, Sama, Yajur and Atharva Vedas.* The ten principal *Upanishads* are known to be the

Isa, the *Kena,* the *Katha,* the *Prasana,* the *Mundak,* the *Mundukya,* the *Taittiriya,* the *Aitereya,* the *Chandogya, and* the *Brhdaranyaka.*

Upanishads as Defined

The term *Upanishad* means 'sitting down near' the teacher to receive instructions or education. Initially, the *Upanishads* are the records of teachings given by the seers (teachers) to their disciples. As time passed, the term *Upanisad* came to mean 'what was received by the teacher.' Max Muller holds that originally *Upanishads* meant 'session', consisting of pupils sitting at a respectful distance around their teacher. Some foreign writers opine that the word '*Upanishad*' means 'secret instructions'. Dr Radha Krishnan states that the term *Upanishad* means 'knowledge which eradicates error and helps one to reach the realm of truth. Samkara, in his 'Introduction to the Commentary on *Taittiriya Upanishad'* states that *Upanishad* means 'True Knowledge of Brahman' because it leads a person to the realm of God and makes him/her free from the bonds of conception, birth and death etc. The *Upanishads* are also known as *Vedanta*, which means *Ved-Ant* or 'End or essence of the *Vedas*' *and* are also a great source to Indian philosophy.

Divergent Meanings Implicit in the Upanishads

In the history of Indian philosophy, the *Upanishads* represent the age when Indian philosophy, initially originating from the *Vedas,* passed through many narrow and difficult grounds, divided itself into many undercurrents and found a suitable outlet in the *Upanishads.* Thus, in the development of thought from the *Vedas* to the *Upanishads,* it is natural to discover wide divergence in thought.

This sort of divergence can be viewed in the following manner and form:

1. Divergence in the Practical Aspect

In the evolution of thought from the *Vedas* to the *Upanishads,* the seers looked more to the practical aspect of attaining self-realization. So far it had been more ritualistic and extrovert. Therefore, spiritual practices that were extrovert in the *Vedas* were directed towards internal experience during the *Upanishadic* period to attain self-realization.

2. Pursuit of Religion Becomes more Subjective

Vedic hymns are more in praise of the natural powers identified as different Gods and Goddesses. *Vedic* seers wondered at the variety of the creation and therefore they worshipped natural powers as Gods. But the seers in the *Upanishads* discovered that God was implicit in one's soul. ***So, it led them to practise concentration and meditation more, than just praying and involving in external rituals. This aspect is seconded in the Kathopanishad, wherein the seers reflect that human mind, being naturally extrovert, is likely to wander recklessly. Therefore, it must be led to introversion to discover the Ultimate Truth and endless happiness by practising concentration and meditation. It is also one of the missions of real education.***

3. Imagination is Substituted by Reasoning

The *Vedic* philosophy is totally implicit with imagination of the seers. In the *Upanishads,* 'thought and reasoning' are considered more important and replace 'imagination and emotion' contained in the *Vedas*. ***The seers during Upanishadic times aimed more at the inquiry of truth. Their goal of life was not to please Gods and Goddesses but to attain self-realization within and without.***

To a great extent it is also the goal of good education that human being must seek truth in all walks of life and discover it by means of meditation and concentration. Since human mind is more or less extrovert, it is likely to wander in quandary. There is more or less only onc way to avoid that sort of reckless wandering, which is unfruitful to humans at all stages of life. It is concentration as well as meditation that can bestow clarity to mind and bring self-realization.

4. Unambiguous Moral Purpose

The Vedic thought has also a moral purpose but a moral purpose appears to be more open in the *Upanishads*. The final goal of life according to the *Upanishads* is the realization of the soul and not merely praying to Gods. The *Upanishadic* seers aim neither at science nor at philosophy but to develop a vital life possessing moral order of the highest kind. Although there is a departure in the way of thinking and doing in the *Upanishads* but the seers always keep faith with the past. They gradually liberate the *Vedic* ideology from ritualism. *Upanishadic* seers are mystic philosophers. Therefore, self-realization is the end of everything in life for them. In view of that *monistic ideology* is considered more relevant and important in the form of *Sachchidananda* in the *Upanishads*.

Main Issues in the *Upanishads*

As time passed and experience became richer, the seers of the *Upanishads* wanted to achieve the summit of knowledge on the basis of their personal experience and knowledge. So they tried to discover the answers to so many difficult questions not properly answered so far by the *Vedas*. These issues were:

1. Search for One in Many

They gradually concluded that behind the multiple forms and phenomena contained in the universe there was some sort of reality which could help one's mind and senses to attain peace. Thus, *Upanishadic* inquiry begins at the dissatisfaction relating to the existing order of things in nature. The seers conceived that our senses did not give us the real knowledge and the mind always moved among dualities. Thus, the search of man from One in Many was the natural urge. The *Mundak Upanisad* reflects: "What is that by the knowledge of which all this can be." (I 1.3)

2. What is Left After Death?

The *Upanishadic* seers were curious to learn more truth about what remained after death. Thus, behind the inquiries into rebirth, soul, and the consequences of man's actions etc., the basic question that confronted them, was, "What is that which remains after death? Wherefrom man has come and whereto will he go?" One of the seers of *Upanishads* reflected candidly, "What is real root from where, in spite of being repeatedly caught by death, the tree of life springs again and again?"

3. What is the Ultimate Reality?

The *Upanishads* were in constant search to know 'what is the Ultimate Reality?' in terms of the physical and mental world. Sometimes it is known as "*prana*" and sometimes "mind". But at other sometimes it is understood as "reason" and sometimes as "soul". Similar more questions relating to man, pervaded the seers' mind. They also wanted to learn, "What is that which remains even when the body is in the sleeping stage and which is constantly creating?" (*Katha Upanishad,* II.5 4.8.) In the field of psychology the *Upanishadic* seers wanted to know "the nature of reality about man regarding what was existent in the stages of his life—walking, dreaming and sleeping..." Thus, the *seers* also tried to know the original cause, the creator, the sustainer, the destroyer of the world.

4. How to Interpret the Truth in Life?

The problems that the seers during the Upanishadic period looked at were not only of practical, moral or religious nature but many of those were also related to everyday life. They aimed at attaining knowledge about the truth and also about its realization and how it could be attained and interpreted in the integral life? Therefore, the seers prayed to the Almighty 'to deliver them from ignorance to truth, from darkness to light and from death to immortality.' This sort of thought is deeply connected with education as it also aims to help humans to attain truth about life and lead it pragmatically by understanding its true meaning.

Upanishads—Inspiration to Indian Thought Systems

Bloomfield writes that, "There is no important form of Hindu thought, heterodox Buddhism included, which is not rooted in the *Upanishads.*" Samkhya-Yoga, Nyaya-Vaisesika, Vedanta, Jainism, etc.—all derive their basic principles from the *Upanishads.* Let us examine this carefully.

(a) Buddhism and Upanishads

One of the leading Western thinkers, Oldenberg, suggests that Buddhism was highly inspired by the *Upanishads.* The precepts of *Karma,* an important thought process in *Upanishads*, became the source of inspiration to most important ideas advanced by the Buddha. Besides, there were many other ideas which directly inspired Buddhism. These are:

(i) *Ritualism* has its source in *Chandogya Upanisad* where in the beginning *Asat* and later on *Sat* comes out to be accepted an important principal of life.

(ii) The *theory of no-soul* in Buddhism also finds its source in *Upanishads.* In *Kathopanisad*, it has been reflected that at the death of a man people think differently about his/her soul. Some consider that it has still some existence, but there are others who reckon that its existence has totally ended.

(iii) Two important Buddhist principles that *there is misery in life* and *all who are born must die* are taken from the *Upanishads*.

(iv) The Buddhist *idea of rebirth* takes its roots from the *Upanishads*. In *Kathopanisad* it is clearly indicated that the souls assume new bodies according to their actions and knowledge.

(v) Also the precept that *everything in this world has its origin in consciousness,* which is one of the principal thoughts in the Buddhist philosophy, owes its origin to the *Upanishads.*

(vi) *The system of monasteries* which occupied an important way of life in Buddhist tradition is also traced back to *Upanishads*, where it is stated that the man who stops attachment toward the world should transcend and start living as a hermit. It gave an idea to the Buddhist monks to live in monasteries.

(b) Samkhya and Upanishads

Like Buddhism *Samkhya Darshan* also owes much to *Upanishads*. Certain precepts of *Samkhya* philosophy can be traced even to the earlier *Upanishads.* Let us examine it carefully:

(i) Concept of Prakrti

The idea of *Prakrti* with its three *Gunas* can be traced to the *Svetasvatra Upanisad,* where it is stated that initially the *Prakrti* contained three colours—red, white and black

(ii) Concept of Purusa

One can trace the idea of *Purusa* and *Mahat* in the *Kathopanisad. Purusa* along with *Prakrit* are major beliefs in *Samkhya* philosophy.

(iii) Astral Body

The idea of astral body found in Samkhya can be traced to the *Upanishads* where different elements of the *Purusa* have been detailed. Thus, *Samkhya* also owes much to them.

(c) Upanishads and Yoga

Most of the y*ogic* philosophy is found in the *Svetasvatra Upanisad.* Various elements like the *Asan*, the *Pranayam,* the *Pratyahar,* the *Dharana* and the *Dhyana*, all preparatory to *Samadhi* and the way to spiritual realization contained in y*oga*, are found in the *Upanishads.* The relation of yoga and the *Upanishads* is intimately found in the aspects of *Dhyana* and God. In the aspect of *Dhyana* in the yogic exercises, one is asked to search for God in one's heart by concentrating upon Him. The God of *Yoga* is said to be beyond all miseries of the world, is just like the sun, the eye of the world. Similarly, the description of the physical aspects in *Yoga*, is also adopted from the *Upanishads*.

(d) Naya Vaisesika and the Upanishads

Like *Yoga, Naya Vaisesika* also owes much to the *Upanishads* for borrowing some of its important aspects of philosophy although one can see sufficient distinction in the two. Some aspects which seemed to have been taken from the *Upanishads* by *Naya Vaisesika* can be seen as follows:

(i) Puritat

The concept of *Puritat* in *Naya Vaisesika* seems to have been borrowed from the *Brhadaranyaka Upanisad* (II. 1.19.) where it is used profusely.

(ii) Categories

The five elements, the soul, mind, time, and ether that are mentioned in the *Vaisesika* philosophy are already mentioned in the *Svetasvatara Upanisad* (II. 2)

(iii) Quality of Akasa

The concept of the quality of *Akasa,* which has been mentioned earlier in the *Chandogya Upanisad, seemed to have been borrowed from it by Vaisesika* philosophy.

(iv) Liberation

The popular concept of liberation is also taken from the *Upanishads* by the Nyaya *Vaisesika* philosophy. Thus, *Nyaya Vaisesika* philosophy also owes much to the *Upanishads* for its major concepts which are considered important features in it.

(e) Mimamsa School of philosophy is almost based upon ritualism and external practices. On the contrary the philosophy in the *Upanishads* follows the path to seek knowledge. Therefore, there is not much similarity in the two. But the aspect of the synthesis of knowledge, taken and explained by Kumarila in *Mimamsa,* is almost similar to what is found in the *Isavasyopanisad.*

(f) Advaita Vedanta and the Upanishads

Most of the *Vedanta* Philosophy is based upon the *Brahma Sutra*, the *Gita* and the *Upanishads*. It will be clearer by an analysis of the *Vedanta* as projected by Samkara and Ramnujam. Samkara's monistic philosophy is completely based upon the *Upanishads*. Some of the basic tenets which are common with *Upanishads* and that of the *Advaita* are as follows.

(i) Brahman, not this, not this

Brahman has been identified without any qualities in the *Upanishads*, though He is the substance (like a solid rock) of the universe and all pervading. In the *Brhadaranyak Upanisad*, Yajnavalka, while discussing the matters related to the universe, points out to his wife Maitreyee, that "Whatever exists in this world is self only." He further identifies *Brahman* or self as the knower, "Who can know that who knows everyone? He is the eternal knower by whom can he be known?" Thus, self (atman) and the *Brahman* are one and the same.

Similarly, Samkara's doctrine regarding *Brahman* and *Atman* is also based upon the *Upanishads*. To Samkara *Atman* and the *Brahman* are not separate. In the *Chandogya Upanisad* (Ch, III 14.4) the soul and *Brahman* are totally identified with each other. It says, "The soul living in the body is really the *Brahman* and as soon as it transcends this worldly frame, it merges with the *Brahman*."

(ii) Doctrine of Maya

The idea and the doctrine of *Maya* propounded by Samkara, has also been taken from the *Upanishads*. Ignorance, *asatya,* blindness, death, non-existence, falsehood, illusion, *Prakrit*, reflections, name and form etc., are mentioned in the *Upanishads* to describe the world.

Some learned thinkers also reckon that even the very word *Maya*, has been taken from the *Upanishads*.

(g) Ramanujam's Qualified Monism

The philosophy of Ramanujam is also based on the *Upanishads* like that of Samkara. The truth is that both Samkara and Ramanujam viewed *Upanishads* from their own angles and supported different sections of *Upanishads* to confirm their own views. At the same time they interpreted other sections of the *Upanishads* according to their own conception of reality. Thus, we find at several occasions the roots of Ramanujam's philosophy in the *Upanishads* like that of Samkara's. Some of them are:

(i) Trinity, the Ultimate Reality

Ramanujam has taken the trinity of *Jiva, Prakrit* and *Isvara* as the Ultimate Reality. This kind of trinity has already been reflected in the *Svetasvatar Upanisad* (I.1.), where it states, "There are three ultimate realities which are all eternal and indestructible and together constitute *Brahman,* viz., the ignorant powerless *Jiva*, all powerful and omniscient God, and eternal *Prakrit* made for the enjoyment of the Jiva and by which it attains fruits of its actions."

(ii) The Pantheism

During discussions relating to the nature of Reality contained in the *Brhadaranyaka Upanisad*,(III.7.) Yajnavalkya and Aruni describe God possessing all powers. "He is all-pervading in the Universe." This pantheistic idea is the basis of Ramanujam's philosophy. He takes God as the soul of *Prakrit.* Yajnavalkya conceives God as the soul of both the world and the *Jiva*. Such references are also found in the *Taittriya Upanisad.*

(iii) God as the Soul of Living and Non-living

According to *Brhadaranyaka Upanisad* (II,5.15), God is the soul of everything, living and non-living. "Just like the spokes of a wheel that are bound with its axel, all the living beings, all the Gods of the world, all souls, are centred in God, Who is the mind of all."

(iv) The Conception of Liberation

Ramanujam's idea of human freedom can be traced to the *Mundaka Upanisad,* where in it is reflected, "When the devotee sees the *Purusa* having golden complexion, the door of all, controller of all and the eternal source of the universe, he quits both the merits and demerits and become one with the divine form, thus, becoming liberated." Similarly, according to the *Mudaka Upanisad* (III.2.6), "When man is established in the *Brahman* consciousness, he becomes free from all sins and reaches the land of *Brahman.* Thus, Ramanujam accepts gradual liberation and liberation by the attainment of divine form.

Methods of the *Upanishads*

The seers during the time of *Upanishads* utilized various methods in their discussions and teachings to know the Truth. Some of the methods are still very relevant to our system of education currently and are greatly helpful for the growth of the teacher and the students as well. The main methods to attain the Truth followed by them are listed below:

(a) The Unfathomable Method

The best illustration of the Unfathomable or Enigmatic Method is found in the *Svetasvatar Upanisad*(1.4), where the nature of realty is found out by a circular kind of method of discussion, they called it an Enigmatic Method. "The Reality is like a great circumscribing felly whose tires are three *Gunas—Sattva, Rajas* and *Tamas*, connected at the end with sixteen *Kalas*, whose spokes are the fifty *Bhavas* or conditions (as indicated by Samkhya philosophy), whose counter spokes are ten senses and their ten objects, whose six sets of eights are such as eight *Dhatus,* the eightfold *Prakrit* and so on. Thus, the Enigmatic Method goes on and on until the seers feel satisfied that they have known the Reality.

(b) Aphoristic Method

This method has been quite widely used by the *Upanisadic* seers in their later philosophical discourses. In this method knowledge is compressed in small general (aphoristic) sentences, which require sufficient intelligence to understand them. It is because of this that the same sentences have been interpreted differently by different commentators. In the *Mandukya Upanisad*, it is stated that the term '*OM*' consists of all that exists, includes all the past, the present and future, and all that which transcends time. Then there is another statement. It says, "Verily, all this is *Brahman*, the *Atman* is *Brahman*. It is four-footed. The first foot is the *Vaiswaner* who enjoys gross things in the state of wakefulness. The second foot is *Taijas*, who enjoys exquisite (lovely) things in the state of dream. The third is *prajna,* who enjoys bliss in the state of deep sleep and the fourth is the *Atman* who is alone, without a second, calm, holy and tranquil. This passage has been interpreted differently in the varied systems of the *Vedantic* philosophy.

(c) Etymological Method

In the Etymological (linguistic) method, the meaning of a word is explained according to its root. For example, in the *Brhadaranyaka*

Upanisad, it is told that 'Purusa' is derived from 'Purisaya' which means inhabiting the heart. Such examples are countless in the *Upanishads*.

(d) Mythical Method

The seers while teaching used it often. In the *Kena Upanishad*, the parable of Indra and the demons has been narrated to preach humility. Sometimes a myth is introduced to highlight a transcendental purpose. For example, in the *Aitereya Upanisad* it is explained how the *Atman* entered the human skull and was individualized as the human soul. Thus, most myths are introduced just to provide moral teaching or for similar purposes.

(e) Analogical Method

Matters that cannot be explained by reasoning are reflected through analogy. By providing similar stories to justify gods' or men's ways, stories are created by the seers to highlight their point of view. Just for example, Yajnavalkya introduces the analogy of the drum in order to explain how the self gets apprehensions.

(f) Dialectical Method

The dialectic method is one of the most widely and accepted methods of the ancient seers. In this method the seers and the thinkers would assemble at one place and discuss different problems among themselves. In the *Upanishads* the use of open discussions has been indicated at several places.

(g) Synthetic Method

Often the dialectical method would follow the synthetic method. In the fourth chapter of the *Brhadaranyaka Upanisad*, Yajnavalka puts to synthesis several issues that are put forward by the Raja

Janak. Similar examples are found in several *Upanishads* including the *Chandogya, Prasna,* and other *Upanishads.*

(h) Monologic Method

It is one of the unique methods used by the seers of the *Upanisadic* times. Though they speak very seldom in their own person, yet they do speak by forgetting the presence of others and go on talking to themselves for a long time. For example, in the *Brhadaranyaka Upanisad,* Yajnavalkya when replying to the questions of Raja Janak regarding the nature of the self, is often lost in self-speech. Similarly, in the *Kathopnisad,* when Yama and Nachiketa discuss matters about self and human nature, Yama goes on talking to himself for a quite long time while replying to various questions posed by Nachiketa.

(i) Ad hoc Method

The seers during *Upanishadic* period taught their disciples in line with their mental and physiological levels. In the *ad hoc* or *temporizing method* the teacher not only shows the pupil the path ahead, but also tells him the whole truth gradually as his spiritual level rises. **This method has been widely accepted by the modern educationists throughout.** During the well known parable of Indra and Virochana, Virochana is satisfied by the first answer of his teacher Prajapati, but Indra is not satisfied. So he goes on asking him about the secret of the soul. Then Prajapati tells him soul's secret that first it is felt in the body and then in the dreams and sleeping stages. After that he explains to him the real nature of the soul. As the enquirer struggles to know the truth, the teacher simply guides him. **Thus, this method is very important for the pupil's spiritual growth.**

(j) Regressive Method

This method is adopted by the seers in the form of many successive questions. Every new question carries the pupil at the back of the previous answer. Thus, when Janak asked Yajnavalkya about the light of man, he answered that it was the sun. Then Yajnavalkya kept Janak engaged by keeping him going to the previous question and its answer and so on until the discussion ended at the *Atman*. Thus, in the *Upanishads*, regressive method has been used very successfully to explain questions and to clarify doubts of the pupils. It is also one of the most agreeable methods accepted by the modern educationists.

Thus, by using varied methods of inquiry to discover the truth, the *Upanishadic* seers tried very intelligently to dispel the doubts of their pupils and guided them to the right path to attain knowledge. Almost all the methods of Upanishads explained above are basically good for modern teachers to adopt and help dispel ignorance among their pupils studying in different fields of knowledge, if they adopt them sincerely and correctly.

Upanishadic Metaphysics

The *Upanishadic* seers pursued the metaphysical problems throughout their lives. Thus, one finds a gradual evolution in the knowledge about the Ultimate Reality. The seers developed the Philosophy of the *Upanishads* by their constant and continual inquiry from generation to generation to discover the nature of the spirituality and the Ultimate Truth.

Prof. Ranade thinks that the metaphysical problem of the *Upanishads* was a cosmological-theological-cum-psychological problem. The Seers first started to know 'how the world was created?' as they took it to be the Ultimate Reality in the beginning. When they were not totally satisfied in their search in the cosmic field, they tried to know the meaning of the Ultimate Reality from the religious standpoint and later on from the psychological standpoint. At this point that they felt satisfied as they thought that they had discovered the meaning of the self. It was later on that they realized that the meaning of truth attained from the psychological process was the same what they had discovered from the religious and cosmological standpoints. They finally concluded that the metaphysical problem regarding the knowledge of the ultimate reality 'was the knowledge of the Self, or the Nature or God.' The Ultimate Reality is only one, the sacred Brahman. Thus, the metaphysical problem of the *Uapnisads,* finally ended in mysticism.

(i) The *Brahman*

The seers discovered that *Brahman* was the essence that pervaded the whole living and non-living world. In the parable of the fruit of the *Nyagrodh* tree in the *Chandogya Upanishad*, it is this principle that has been explained lucidly. In view of the parable, the physical world is the external manifestation of that subtle essence. The soul is the essence of all things. Thus, there is only one essence behind both, Mind and Nature. Metaphysically both are one and the same.

Besides the cosmic field, when the seers searched for the Ultimate Reality in the spiritual field, they started with the discussions about the gods and goddesses that the Vedas had discovered earlier. As the idea of one God ultimately came to the minds of the *Upanishadic* seers, the importance of various gods and goddesses decreased. They concluded that the self was also identified with this God of gods. In the *Brhadaranyaka Upanishad* (III.8.9), during the discussion between Yajnavalkya and Vidagdha Sakalya, it is concluded after much thought that *Brahman* alone is the God of the Universe and His body is the earth, his physique is the fire and his mind is the night, which is the ultimate end of all human souls. He is the creator, the sustainer and the destroyer of the universe. He is the master of all, the omnipresent and the omnipotent. Nature and time are guided by Him. He is the only Knower. He possesses all the qualities. He is beyond the present, the past and the future. His power is expressed before us in the form of knowledge and motion. He is neither cause nor effect but the only cause of everything. The powers of Nature are only powers of *Brahaman*. All the elements are born in Him. All of them live in Him and finally culminate in Him.

'*Regarding Brahman as knowledge*' has already been explained. The *Upanishadic* seers arrived at the truth that self-consciousness is the ultimate reality. Self-consciousness is the directing power of the eyes, the ears, the nose, the mind and everything else. It is beyond mind and intellect. In the well-known sentences 'That Thou Art', 'I am Brahman', 'All is Brahman', etc., the fact is explained that self-consciousness is the essence of the whole universe. It is the self and also the *Brahman.*

Yajnavalkya explains self-consciousness further: 'If self-consciousness is not possible then nothing is possible at all.' It is true that the *Brahman* cannot be known by the senses, mind or intellect, yet it is the object of immediate experience. The *Upanishads* holds two forms of the *Brahman, Para and Apara. Para* is higher while *Apara* is lower. *Para Brahman* is infinite, attribute-less, unconditioned, without names, forms and transcendent. The *Apara* is limited, attributed, conditioned, with name and form, and is immanent. The first, Para, is beyond space, time, causality and the world; the second,

Apara, is the master of the universe and entangled in cause and effect relationship. It is God. Both, *Para and Apara Brahman* are two aspects of the same *Brahman.*

(ii) The World

Upanishads consider that the world is the manifestation of the *Brahman.* The *Brahman* creates the world and then takes it back inside, just like a spider, which creates its web and then goes back inside it. He does not create the world out of something as there was no matter before creation. There was only one soul before creation. He then decided to create the world and created it. He created the subtle and the gross, the formless and with forms. Ether was born out of self, air from ether, fire came out of air, water from fire, the earth from water and finally from the earth came out the plants etc. Thus, the world was already in the *Brahman* in the un-manifested form. He manifested it, created the names and forms and also the objects. All, space, time, nature, etc., are covered by the *Brahman.* Just as the plants are born on the earth, hair come out of the body, similarly the world comes out of the perfection of the *Brahman* and returns into Him. The rivers, oceans, mountains, plants, human beings, animals, birds, the four *Vedas,* and *Karmas*, including gods have originated from the *Brahman.* In the *Svetasvatara Upanisad* (I.1), *Brahman* has been addressed as '*Isa*'. He is also called Siva, *Rudra, Hara and Maheswar.* The individual self is implicit with ignorance and sub-ordinate, but God is the Master of the universe. Nature, individual self and God are separate from one another. The truth is that the *Brahman* manifests Himself through three forms, the experiencing individual, the phenomenal world and also God, Who guides both to create worldly experience in the individual self.

God creates the world through His power of *Maya* or *Prakriti*. *Prakriti* is dynamic and is one with *Satya, Rajas* and *Tamas*. It creates things through these three *Gunas*. Thus, God creates the universe by His power and rules over it as the controller of the *Gunas*.

(iii) The *Jiva* or *Atman*

The *Upanishads* hold that the individual self and the Supreme self reside in the same heart of the same body like darkness and light. The first has been called as the *Jiva* and the second as *Atman*. The *Jiva* suffers the consequences of its actions and also feels pleasure and sustains pain, while the self is beyond all such things. The *Jiva* suffers pain on account of its ignorance. By the knowledge contained in the self, the ignorance (dualism) and is wiped out. In fact *Jiva* is different (and beyond) from the body, mind, intellect and senses. It is the knower, the enjoyer, and the doer and is conscious eternally. It is without beginning and end, but it does not possess infinite knowledge. It is beyond birth and death. It also does not die with the body and has the freedom of will. But it is caught in bondage on account of ignorance and actions committed on that account. It gets merits and demerits, pleasure and pain according to its good and bad actions. It is subject to re-birth, which takes place according to its *Karmas*. Broadly speaking *Jiva* has four stages. These are:

(a) Walking stage which *Jiva* is called *Vaiswaner,* who enjoys the worldly pleasures through external senses.

(b) Dreaming stage in which *Jiva* is known as '*Taijasa*', who knows the subtle internal objects and enjoys through the mind.

(c) Sleeping stage, in which *Jiva* is known as '*Prajna*', in which one is uniform, conscious and blissful and does not perceive internal objects.

(d) Turyia stage in which *Jiva* is known as *Atman* which is neither conscious nor un-conscious, but one, non-dual, and possesses universal consciousness. This *Atman* is *Brahman.*

Jiva is within the five (*Sheaths* or covers) subtle bodies, which are:

(a) Physical Sheath or *Annamaya Kosa* has a form, which possesses sense organs and a body which are maintained through this sheath.

(b) Vital *Sheath or Pranmaya Kosa* is within the physical self, is full of energy that creates motion in the body and is sustained through it (energy).

(c) Mental *Sheath* or *Manomaya Kosa* is within the vital *sheath* and depends upon the mind which causes selfish desires.

(d) Consciousness *Sheath* or *Vijnanamaya Kosa* which is within the mental sheath or cover and depends upon the intellect and its activities.

(e) Bliss *Sheath* or *Anandmaya Kosa* is within the conscious *sheath*, is full of bliss and has no distinction of subject. It is finite, transcendent and perfect, and is not a cover of the self but its essence. This self is the real essence of the *Jiva* or *Brahman*. It is through the knowledge of *Brahman* its bondage is loosened. This knowledge is attained through its direct experience. In the *Kathopanisad* this self is identified as the Ultimate Reality, is mortal, self-evident and self-enlightened. According to the *Kathopanisad* (II.2.15), 'It is by the shining of the self that everything else shines, it is by its light that all this is lighted.

(iv) Bondage and Freedom

The *Upanishads* hold that ignorance is the cause of bondage and liberation is the result of knowledge. Ignorance creates delusion, egoism and plurality. It is intellectual knowledge that provides the distinction between subject and object. It is through this real knowledge which one gets freedom or liberation and the bondage of transmigration is finally broken. This knowledge is obtained through immediate experience, which is beyond intellectual knowledge, which is the field of higher knowledge and is obtained through identity.

It is ignorance which gives birth to ego. As a result, the *Jiva* identifies itself with the sense organs, mind, intellect and body. Attachment to the physical world creates bondage, which is primarily caused by egoism, selfishness and attachment to the objects. When ego is totally destructed, the *Jiva* realizes its real nature by identification itself with the *Brahman,* the bondage disappears. It is the real identity of the *Jiva* with the *Brahman* having no desire of merit or fear of demerit, no attachment, no state of pleasure or pain etc. It is the state of eternal peace and total bliss.

Perhaps there is no better idea than fostering non-attachment by removing ignorance that leads to unnecessary human desires. It could be cultivated in our students through right kind of knowledge provided to them by our teachers and school curriculum so that they may live in peace and harmony and may let others also live in peace. It is one of the best thoughts propounded by the Upanishadic seers. It can be fostered among our students by clarifying before them through various curricular activities like community services and exposing them to certain odd and difficult situations from time to time so that they may be enlightened and try to abandon greed and lust and live with

contentment and harmony with others, irrespective of different religious backgrounds .

The Upanishads have not only discussed the nature of bondage and freedom but also have discovered means to achieve liberation. To possess knowledge of the Brahman is to become one with Him. In that respect the Upanishads have also discussed in detail the means to achieving liberation or to attain the Brahman. All this is highly related to education during all times and has been one of the important missions of education as liberation from ignorance and attainment of freedom can never be excluded from the realm of contemporary education too.

Attainment of Spiritual Realization

The *Upanishads* hold strongly that without fulfilling certain conditions one should not hope to attain liberation. These conditions are as follows:

(i) Concentration on the Inner Self

One of the conditions to attain liberation or self-realization is to *stop running after the worldly objects* though it is the innate desire of all human beings. To be away from that desire, the mind needs to concentrate on the inner soul by restraining that tendency and try hard to take away the senses from the external objects.

(ii) Purification

The *Kathopanisad* holds that the self cannot be released by merely talking about religious matters or through intellectual exercises or by listening spiritual tales. The *Mundaka Upanisad* states that strictness, truth, real knowledge and the life of celibacy are the prerequisites to attain self-realization.

(iii) Teacher's Role

The *Kathopanishad* commenting on 'how a teacher can help in attaining the freedom from the delusion' reflects: 'Arise, Awake and learn from those who are better than you, because the path of self-realization is difficult like the edge of the knife.' (Kath iv.9.3) Similarly, in the *Chandogya Upanisad*, through the parable of the man living in the country of Gandhar, it has been clearly stated that the need of a teacher to guide one along the path of self-realization is great. Such *Upanishadic* reflections are closely related to the field of education.

(iv) Dedication to God

The *Svetasyatar Upanishad* reflects clearly that unless the pupil does not possess sufficient devotion to God and faith in the teacher he/she can't be redeemed and reach the path of self-realization. If the pupil has full devotion to God, leads a life of celibacy, meditates properly, he/she can proceed to the path of self-realization after initiation from the teacher. There are two important aids to follow this path—one is the practice of yoga and the other is the concentration on 'Om' according to the *Upanishads*. When these paths are followed properly, the self becomes one with the *Brahman*.

Certainly some of these ideas and ways could still be very useful to our students at all levels of schooling. The idea is not simply to lead a life of celibacy but to be free from greed, unwanted anti-social activities and free from ignorance that is neither helpful to the self nor to the society. It must be the aim of education during all times to promote self-realization in the sense to help one transcend from one's baseness, hypocrisy, covetousness

and narrow mindedness. In that respect the teacher's role is also very important at all levels of schooling.

The State of Self-Realization

As a consequence of the realization of the five stages to attain spiritual evolution one reaches a unique stage that we call self-realization. In that stage there is the end of physical attachment and desires, end of doubts and desires, acquisition of great strength, state of absolute bliss, no fear of any kind, and all desires satisfied. This is the real state of self-realization.

Questions

1. Name the methods of teaching used by the Upanishadic seers to enlighten their pupils about the important issues relating to human life? Describe briefly any three of them?
2. Which of the methods used by the Indian seers Samkara and Ramanujam during the Upanishadic period are highly relevant to our modern system of education and can help students grow fruitfully?
3. What procedures have been identified by the Upanishadic seers for the spiritual realization of human beings? Is there any relevance of such procedures in the field of modern education to help students to attain the required moral values?
4. Describe briefly the difference in meaning of the terms Jiva and Atman as proposed by the seers during Upanishadic period.

5. It is believed that the Upanishadic thought process has been greatly inspirational to the Buddhist, Samkhya and Advaita Vedanta systems of Indian philosophy? What aspects of Upanishadic thought have been adopted by Samkara and Ramanujam in building their philosophical ideologies?
6. What steps have been identified by the Upanishadic seers to attain the spiritual realization? How those ideas could be useful to our students in the realm of education in the modern times?

Chapter Four

The Philosophy Contained in the Bhagwad Gita

Historical Backdrop

The exact date of the composition of the *Mahabharata* is not known with certainty. Therefore the Gita's date of composition is also not very definite. According to different scholars like C.V. Vidya and Tarakeshwar Bhattacharya, the war of the *Mahabharata* was supposedly held either in 3102 B.C. or 1432 B.C. In view of that the Gita could have been composed around 2000 to 3000 B.C. There is also a lot of disagreement about the number of couplets in the Gita. Some thinkers hold that the original Gita did not include 700 couplets that are found in the present versions, and that many others were included after the Mahabharata war took place.

Importance of *Gita* for the People

As the modern age is implicit with scientific inventions and new ideas in that direction, some hold that there is not much advantage to study the *Gita*. But on the contrary it is the present age when there is a dire need to study the *Gita*. The *Gita* is based upon the fundamental principles of human nature and therefore, it will always be the source of inspiration to human beings. People like Mahatama Gandhi, Tilak and many foreigners have greatly been influenced by the *Gita's* message, that primarily teaches how to lead a sane life when one is surrounded by turmoil, tragedies and disappointments. In modern times when every effort to bring about world peace seems to be futile, the Gita's teaching of world brotherhood may be of great guidance to humanity. The Gita holds that the ultimate end is the consolidation of society and reflects the liberality which characterizes Indian thought.

The *Gita*'s Relation to the Upanishads

It has been traditionally well known that the *Gita* contains the spirit of *Upanishadic* philosophy but the Upanishads are so subtle and deep that they are beyond ordinary men's understanding. It is the *Gita* alone that helps ordinary persons to understand their duties and responsibilities in life though it reflects the same views as contained in the *Upanishads.* The similarities between the two are:

1. The *Atman* is Never Born nor is Killed

The *Kathopanishad* (1.2.18) holds that the Atman is never born nor is killed; never comes from anything nor becomes anything; it is unborn; imperishable, has existed from all eternity, and is not killed when the body is killed." Similarly, at another place the Gita repeats almost what has been stated in the *Kathopanisad* (1.2.19) about the *Atman.* "When a killer thinks he is killing and the killed takes that he is being killed, neither of them knows that they are wrong for the *Atman* is neither killed nor ever killing." These verses have exactly been repeated in the Chapter II verse 19 in the *Gita.*

The following verse has also almost been taken from the *Kathopanishad* (1.2.7) by the *Gita* and repeated in its Chapter II in verse 29: "The *Atman* is not even so much as heard of by many so that even after hearing him, people do not know him, that the seeker of atman is a miracle, that the obtainer of him must have exceeding insight....”

2. ‘OM’ Inspires Spiritual Discipline

The *Bhagavad-Gita* reproduces verbatim the following verse from the *Kathopanishad* (1.1.15) in its Chapter VIII in verse 13. It says: “What words the Vedas declare, the ascetics busy themselves about, what word inspires the life of spiritual discipleship... that word briefly is *OM*’

3. God’s and Brahman’s Path are Similar

The idea of the path of Gods and the path of fathers being the same, taken from the *Vedas* by the *Upanishads* was literally taken by the *Gita* as reflected in its Chapter VIII verse 24-25. It says: “Those who move by the path of the Gods move towards *Brahman,* while those who go by the path of fathers, return by the path by which they have gone.”

Besides the above the *Gita* has **other ideological similarities** with that of the *Upanishads.*

For example, the importance of devotion and worship has been borrowed from the *Svevtasvatara Upanishad* by the *Gita.* The philosophy of *Karma yoga* in the *Gita* has been borrowed from the *Isavasyopanasad* (II). The description of the cosmic form of God contained in the XIth Chapter of the *Gita* is taken from the *Mundakopanisad* (II.1.), where the cosmic person with fire as his head, the sun and moon as his eyes, the quarters as his ears and the *Vedas* as his speech, air as his *Prana*, etc. Besides, the emotional attitudes and the devotional impulses contained in the *Upanishads* are also present in the *Gita* for they are the basis for the theistic and mystic philosophy of the *Bhagwad Gita.*

But there are points of difference in both the *Gita* and the Upanishads. In the beginning Arjuna requests Sri Krishna to tell him the definite path and in the end he clearly understands his duty and prepares to follow it. In the *Upanishads* there are three paths—of knowledge, action, and devotion, out of which finally the path of knowledge has been established as the best path to follow. In that respect the *Gita* is more practical and seems to be synthesizing better than the *Upanishads.* It is more practical and lays stress on action and devotion. And thus, it has synthesized activism along with renunciation.

The *Niskam Karma*, as the Central Teaching

The *Gita* has been considered as the most important scripture in Indian literature. Therefore, many eminent scholars and philosophers in India have commented upon its theme and tried to propagate their own views through it. **The Gita definitely presents the path of *Niskam Karma*, which is also its central teaching. In spite of various interpretations given by Samkara, Ramanujam, Mahadevan and Ballabhacharya, Tilak and Mahatama Gandhi about its central theme or teaching, the Gita's main interpretation remains steadfast. The truth is that viewing things from a spiritual view point is always the whole and integral. Thus, in the Gita the apparently contradictory paths of knowledge, devotion and action are really complementary to each other. This synthesis is neither a pragmatic compromise, nor a golden mean nor an organic relation. It is the status of spiritual unity which cannot be merely comprehended by intellectual means. Thus, the *Gita* takes man to a stage where all aspects of man's personality are integrated, transformed and divinized. There cannot be a better**

goal of education than making human personality integrated, transformed and divinized.

In order to understand the central teaching of the *Gita* one needs to look into the *Gita* itself. At the end of every chapter in the *Gita*, it has been stated, "the knowledge of Brahman, the science of yoga." Thus, the *Gita* claims to be the science of yoga which it systematically studies. The word Yoga has been derived from the root word '*yuj*' which means union or identity. **According to Sri Krishna, "Yoga is perfection in action." One can attain the ultimate end viz. realization of God or consolidation of society by this means only. As a matter of fact, according to the Gita consolidation of society is an essential aspect of realization of God, and one who has realized God, must work as a divine instrument to achieve the divine purpose. Hence the central teaching of Gita is *Niskama Karma* Yoga. *Niskam* does not mean without personal desire as action without motive is not (psychologically) possible. It means an action in accordance to the divine will.**

Karma in the *Gita* means working according to one's own *Varna* and *Asram.* Since Sri Krishna himself proclaims that he is the initiator of the *Varna* system, the *Gita* has given a divine sanction to the scientific principle of division of labour, which was not based upon heredity but simply based upon one's own temperament and capacity. This action should not be for the individual's desire or *Asram*, but for God alone. Kant's dictum of "duty for duty's sake" is not acceptable in the *Gita*. It teaches "duty for deity's sake". Yoga in the *Gita* means identity with God and identity is the ultimate end of the *Gita.* But this concept of identity is dynamic and man does not become inactive after realization of God. He becomes even more active than before due to his union with the original source of energy. **Thus, *Niskam Karma* is in harmony with the physical, psychological and spiritual nature of man. It harmonizes the good of the individual with that of society. In fact, *Niskam Karma* yoga has a great bearing on our educational system as it suggests action without having any desire for self-fulfilment or personal gains. It helps one to have full faith in God, surrender totally unto Him and think fruitfully to help fellow beings.**

Metaphysics in the Gita

The Concept of God

The *Gita* holds that there are two kinds of realities in the world. One is perishable and the other is imperishable, the first is *Prakrti* and the second, *Atman*. Beyond these and underlying both is God, known as *Purusottama,* who is transcendent and immanent as well. He is the sustainer of the world, the source of everything here and hereafter. (*Gita* IX.17-18-XII.16-18) In Chapter XI, *Gita* addresses God as imperishable, omniscient, the ultimate source of universe, the eternal *purusa*, the first God, the ancient Being, and beginning-less. The Absolute is the God from the point of view of the universe. In the *Gita,* the philosophical aspect of the Divine has not been so much emphasized as His practical aspect. It gives an important place to self-surrender and the more complete is the self-surrender, the nearer the man is to God. Even the most sinful person may attain freedom through devotion to God. The *Gita* also hold that God incarnates even though He is eternal, infinite, beginning-less and transcendent but by limiting his infinity through his power of *Maya* he becomes embodied and descends to human level. Sri Krishna justifies this sort of act (Chapter XII. 12) and states, "Though unborn and immortal and also the Lord of being, I manifest through my *yoga* (divine power), keeping my nature under control…" He says further, "Whenever there is decline of *Dharma* (righteousness), I bring myself forth for the protection of the worthiest, for destruction of the evil and for establishing *Dharma* on a firm footing I take birth from age to age."

The *Gita* always holds its belief in theism. At the end of the Chapter X in the *Gita*, Sri Krishna clearly reflects that, "God is present everywhere in the universe in subtle form and the world exists as a part of Him. As a matter of fact the spiritual phenomena cannot be easily explained through dialectical reasoning. A divine phenomenon is different from a material phenomenon and, therefore, the precepts of the intellectual logic cannot be applied to it. God is perfect both as omniscient God and as supreme person. He is also immanent and transcendent above all. All this can only be understood through immediate spiritual experience.

The Concept of World

God is the efficient cause of the *Prakrit*, which is the material cause of the universe. God's *Prakrit* has two aspects—*Paraa* and *Apara. Apara*, the lower *Prakrit* includes life, water, air, ether, mind and intellect. These are the physical, the vital and the psychological worlds. The *Para Prakrit* which is of higher nature embodies the soul. It is also conscious *Prakrit.* Both are God's power. Therefore, God is the material and efficient cause of the universe. *Prakrit* is the *Maya* of God. It is constituted of three *Gunas*, viz. *Sattva, Rajas* and *Tamas*. God creates the *Jiva,* in view of their merits and demerits. Both *Prakrit* and *Purasa* are eternal not perishable. *Maya* as *Prakrit* is not its real reflection, but creates an illusory image of the *Prakrit.*

The Self

The body is limited in space and time and is born and dies, but the *Jiva* is the eternal part of God. The soul is unborn, immortal, beyond time and space, infinite and eternal. It cannot be described, it is unchanging, all pervading, immovable and actionless and beyond mind, intellect and senses. When the body becomes of no use the soul leaves it and enters a new body. It is completely beyond *Sattva, Rajas* and *Tamas*. Self or soul is beyond *Gunas,* of which pleasure, pain, illusion, emotions, passion, mind, intellect and senses are born. When man reaches the stage of self-realization, he is unaffected by pleasure and pain and in a detached state witnesses all such things. This is the highest state of soul. Knowledge is the essence of soul and by controlling the senses through mind and intellect one may realize the self and reach the Ultimate Truth that is God. God realization is possible only through self surrender. Such a man does not act for God but acts as His instrument. In the *Gita* the ideal man works for the good of all living beings. Thus, the ***Gita holds that man should reach the non-dualistic stage by working spontaneously for Him. Even beyond this is the spiritual field in which all the moral conflicts disappear. Then man can finally establish in the divine consciousness and can act for the good of the people. In this stage there is no egoism of will. Thus, absolute surrender to God is self-realization, which is the final goal of all Indian philosophy, religion as well as ethics.*** Freedom does not mean indetermination but self-determination. When the self becomes one with God, there lies real freedom, as man becomes a divine instrument. Let us now briefly discuss the underlying ethics in the *Bhagwad Gita.*

Ethics in the *Gita*

God-realization is the ultimate goal of man according to the *Gita.* It teaches the *Varnashram Dharma* and its fulfillment becomes a duty as it has been proclaimed by Lord Krishna, Who says that four *Varnas* have been created by Him according to the distinction of qualities and actions. God realization also leads to the knowledge of the nature of soul as it is only a form of God. The soul is to be experienced internally and also in the external world. As God is the controller of self and physical world, the soul is merely an instrument of His purpose.

In a similar way the *Gita* holds that public service is as much important as God realization. **Sri Krishna reflects in the Gita that a yogi who keeps himself busy with the welfare of all beings, goes to Him. Social service pushes man towards God. Duty should be done not simply for duty's sake but for the sake of betterment of the society.**

Niskama Karma

The *Gita* preaches karmayoga which helps man to be free from bondage by keeping himself active. This yoga is also called skill in action. Thus, *Niskama Karma* is not unintentional action but rather an action with an intention of submission to God without possessing any desire of result. Sri Krishna while discussing the meaning of Karma provides various definitions of *Niskama Karma* and enlightens him and us all about it.

In the eighteenth chapter of the Gita Lord Krishna further elaborates the meaning of *Niskama Karma* to Arjuna while advising him to fight as it is his duty to fight against those who

are sinful and who tend to be unjust to others on account of various reasons. He then tells him that a man should pursue his duties according to his own profession and *Varna* and *Asram*. The inherent duty of a Kshatriya is to fight, and therefore, he must fight. To deviate from duty or to do it under obligation is immoral. Only the activity that is done with personal motive and without any free desire has some moral importance. Thus, the Gita has synthesized abstinence and action in an excellent way and has provided a clearer meaning of duty to be performed voluntarily.

Two Types of Elements

In view of the *Gita's* philosophy the world has two kinds of elements—true and false, which are permanent and temporary respectively. Truth cannot be ever destroyed and falsehood is always transitory. The soul is true, indestructible, permanent and immutable. It is not changeable but everything else is changeable, and false. The body is false as it is born and it dies. It is destructible and transitory and which is born, must die. All objects of the world are perishable. None can stop them to take birth and to die.

Virtues

The *Gita* has described the divine qualities or the virtues quite elaborately. Sri Krishna says that one who has virtues he has realized God. The person who has realized God is free from malice, egoism, delight, anger and troubles. He is friendly, forgiving, is compassionate, contented, united with God, keeps control on his body, mind and senses, is impartial, pure, wise and has complete resolve and determination. He is never annoyed

or feels offended, does not rejoice or grieves and possesses no desires. He has no attachments and is full of devotion to God.

Educational Implications

The *Gita* contains a lot that can influence the realm of education during all times. It clarifies how one should follow one's duty according to one's *Varna Ashram* and 'what is the right meaning of *Niskama Karma*?' which is often misunderstood by most of the people even if they read the *Gita* regularly. The meaning of *Varna Ashram* according to the *Gita* is to follow the profession according to one's desire and not according to one's birth in a family. It is so unfortunate that we have gone too far in misunderstanding the meaning of *Varna Ashram*. Consequently we have to bring changes to our constitution time to time to redeem the downtrodden who must not be treated in the manner they were being treated at the time of country's independence. No education can fulfil its obligations towards its pupils if it teaches discrimination. Although much has been done in that direction, yet a lot still needs to be done as people must follow values in the right perspective rather than by the force of the law.

The most important contribution of the *Gita* is the idea of *Niskama Karma* which is also misunderstood by most people even though they read the *Gita* very regularly. The idea of serving society is one of the greatest ideas that any religious book can provide to its people. It can only be done if our education can create such an environment for our students and provide them examples by our teachers whose responsibility in that respect is great. It is not something like Kant's dictum of 'duty for duty's sake' but duty for the society as desired by God. If one is totally

submerged in Him, totally surrenders to God, then whatever he does, is in line with God's desire, and is also right. And God always desires us to help our people. Thus, the *Gita*'s contributions in the field of education is lot if it is adhered to properly. Besides, the *Gita* also elaborately defines the meaning of Virtues. Such virtues are always required and need to be cultivated through our education with the help of the right kind of teachers and good environment of the school.

Questions

1. What is the central teaching of the *Gita*? What are its educational implications? Discuss critically.
2. What is common between the *Gita* and the *Upanishads*? To what extent does the *Gita* differs from the *Upanishads*?
3. What kind of values does the Gita prescribe for a man? How can they be fostered in our current educational environment at school level?
4. To what extent is the meaning of *Niskama Karma* properly understood by most of the people? What is its right meaning contained in the *Gita*? What bearing does it have on our education system?
5. Discuss the ethical views propounded by the *Gita*. How far are those views applicable in modern times?

Chapter Five

Jain Philosophy

Historical Perspective

The Jaina system has a notable place among the heterodox schools of Indian philosophy. The Jains did not believe in the *Vedas*, but admitted the existence of a soul distinct from other elements. They agreed in developing a whole technique of mental control and acquiring right knowledge, right perception and right conduct.

Jaina philosophy was first initiated by Rishabha Deva, along with Ajit Nath and Aristanemi. According to the Jains, these names are found in the *Vedas* and Jaina philosophy, therefore, is said to be very old. While the first Tirthankar was known as Adi Nath, the last Jain Tirthankar was named Vardhaman Mahavir. In between the two, one finds the names of twenty two other Tirthankars, viz., Ajit Nath, Sambhava Nath, Abhinadan, Sumati Nath, Padma Prabhu, Suprashva Nath, Chandra Prabh, Suridhi Nath, Shital Nath, Dharma Nath, Shanti Nath, Muni Subrate, Nemi Nath and Parshva Nath etc. The last Tirthankar, Mahavir, was born in 599 B.C. He became a recluse at the age of thirty, performed hard penances to gain true knowledge. After attaining the Truth, he was called Mahavir and the leader of a group of monks known as Nirgrantha.

Mahavir strongly emphasized the virtue of celibacy, detachment and ordered the monks to relinquish all clothes in order to become absolutely detached from right and wrong. Those who followed this order were named Digambara, while those who wore white clothes, were known as Svetambara. Both of these sects, however, followed the same philosophy and were guided by the teachings of Mahavir. Among Mahavir's disciples were monks as well as laity of both sexes.

After the death of Mahavir, his chief followers managed the Sangha for many years. Bhadra Bahu was the leader in 317 B.C. In 310 B.C., Sthula Bhadra took over from him and organised a congregation for the compilation of Jaina scriptures. It was at this juncture that Jains were divided into two sects of Digambara and Svetambara. Since then, important works on Jaina thought were published by eminent Jaina scholars upto the 17th century. In the field of both knowledge and metaphysics, Jaina philosophy is pluralist and relativist. Jain metaphysics is based on knowledge, so it is necessary to understand epistemology as a prelude to the understanding of their metaphysics.

Categories of Knowledge

Like other philosophical schools, the Jainas have also critically examined the valid sources of knowledge. But *Naya* is a distinctive feature of the Jaina system. According to the Jaina-thinkers, knowledge is of two kinds, viz., *Pramana* and *Naya*. *Pramana* refers to the knowledge of a thing as it is. *Naya* is the knowledge of a thing in a particular context or in relationship with the knower. *Naya*, in other words, is that particular standpoint from which we deliver out judgement about a particular thing. Nayas would thus differ with differing standpoints, and every *naya* gives us relative knowledge.

According to the Jainas, everything possesses an infinite number of qualities (*dharma*). When we affirm a thing by one of these manifold qualities, we apprehend *naya*. But when we know a thing in different ways and through different qualities, this knowledge comes through *pramana*. **Thus both *pramana* and *naya* are essential for the true knowledge of a thing.**

Kinds of *Pramana*

Like other philosophers, the Jainas also divide knowledge gained through *Pramana* into two categories, viz., direct (*Paroksha*) and indirect (*Aparoksha*). But there is only a relative difference between the two. Indirect is only relatively indirect, and direct is only relatively direct. According to Siddhasena Diwakar, *Pramana* is that knowledge which illuminates itself and others without any hindrance. **Therefore, *Pramanas*, both direct and indirect, enlighten themselves as well as others. Obviously, direct knowledge is the correct knowledge of a thing. It is gained by the soul unaided by mind or the sense organs.**

Direct Knowledge

Direct knowledge is either practical (*Vyavharika*) or otherworldly (*Parmarthika*). Otherworldly knowledge is immune from the effect of actions, and illuminates independently without the help of the mind or sense organs. There exists in it a direct connection between the knower and the known. Unless one is free from the shackles of action one cannot have this kind of knowledge. This is genuine knowledge and it is this which sheds light on all the objects of the universe. Practical or mundane knowledge is to be distinguished from the otherworldly, in as much as the former is achieved through the mind and the sense organs. The latter requires no such media. Again, while the former can be acquired by the common folk but the latter cannot be acquired by all.

Mati and Srta Jnana

Direct practical knowledge is of two kinds—*Mati* and *Srta.* Here are the differences between the *Mati* and *Srta* knowledge:

1. In the former, the objects of perception are present, but in the latter the objects may belong to the past, present or future.
2. The latter is related to *Jainagma.* So it is superior to the former.
3. The latter, being the utterance of great ones (*Aptavachana*), is pure and beyond *parinama*, while the former is subject to the effect of *parinama.*

All kinds of substances are known with the help of *Mati* and *Srti.* Concrete substance is the object of *Avadhi Jnana.* Subtle substance is known through *Mati.* In all these four types of knowledge, one cannot know the objects, which are produced by the modifications of substance. The knowledge of *paryayas* is the object of *Kevala jnana.*

Indirect Knowledge

Indirect knowledge is of five kinds—*Smriti, Pratyabhijna, Tarka, Anumana* and *Agam.* These will be now discussed in details.

1. *Smrti* (Memory): To recollect something known directly in the past as a result of the awakening of some impression is known as *Smrti* or memory. Impression (*Samskara*) is a

peculiar capacity of the soul. Not only direct perception of the past, but recollection, recognition, logic and inference of the past also leave impressions upon the soul. So these may also arouse memory. For the Jainas, memory is valid knowledge, because it is the correct form of things perceived in the past.

2. *Pratyabhijna* (Recognition): This is the synthetic knowledge contributed by direct perception and recollection. In it one knows resemblance *(Samanata)*, identity (*Tadatmya*), difference (*Bheda*), comparison (*Tulana*) etc. In it one knows the general (*Samanya*) in the form of similar change (*Sadrsaparinama*) of different *Jivas* and *Ajivas*. Recognition is valid knowledge of a special kind. In it one sees a thing in the present in the form of that which one perceived in the past, e.g. this is that *Deva Dutt*. Direct perception apprehends, 'This'.

3. *Tarka* (Reasoning): *Tarka* is the knowledge of concomitance (*Vypati*) between *Paksa* and *Sadhya*. It depends upon the perception whether two things exist together or not, in the past, the present and the future.

4. *Anumana* (Inference): Inference is the knowledge of *Sadhya* with the help of *hetu*. This inference is either *Svarthanumana* or *pararthanumana*. The former is the inference for one's own self. Hence it needs no amplification. For example, the frequent visibility of fire and smoke together suffices to convince us to their concomitance. Afterwards, when one sees smoke, one infers the existence of fire also with the help of *Vyapti*, which is already known to us.

5. *Agam*: This is the knowledge of something through the words of reliable people. A person, who knows things in their true form, and expresses his views about them correctly, his views are reliable. It is also known as *Apta*. Such a man is free from prejudice. His words simply narrate the truth. *Agam* is of two kinds, viz, Mundane (*laukika*) and Supermundane (*alaukika*). Jains have full faith in the Tirthankaras, who have attained complete perfection as well as realized all knowledge. The Jains don't believe in the Vedas. They hold that as a lamp illuminates a thing, so word also manifests a thing by its inherent power. Therefore, the words of reliable people are not only true but they also provide true knowledge.

Syadvada

Syadvada or Saptabhangi Naya is the most important part of the Jaina logic. Syadvada is neither scepticism nor agnosticism. In fact, Syadvada is the theory of the relativity of knowledge. The form, substance, scope and time of every existing object are understood only in relation to those of some other objects. Therefore, the knowledge of any object is not absolute, but relative.

Anekantavada

According to the Jainas, reality is neither eternal nor ephemeral. It is changeable, but it never loses its own self. Every object has more than one attribute. The Kevali can have direct knowledge of all these different attributes of an object, but an ordinary mortal can see only one object and from one standpoint at a time. So when one considers an object one must keep its different attributes in view. This theory of regarding reality as many-sided, eternal and ephemeral, animate and inanimate etc. is known as *Anekantavada*.

Durnity Naya and Pramana

According to the Jainas, an object can be mainly viewed in three ways. The knowledge, which views the part as the whole, is known as *Durniti*. If knowledge is regarded as it is, without judging it to be either partial or absolute, then it is termed *Naya*. When the knowledge is accompanied by the consciousness then it is limited, relative and conditional and that is can be interpreted in different ways according to different standpoints. It is termed as *Pramana* or *Syad sat*. To denote *Pramana*, the epithet *Syat* must precede *Naya*. *Syat* is supposed to be the sign of truth. It is relative and it has gradual knowledge. *Syat* eliminates the contradiction between divergent standpoints. Rejection of the theory of *Syadvada* is tantamount to the adoption of absolute viewpoint which goes counter to all experience.

According to the Jainas, *pramana* cannot be unconditional and exclusive. Affirmation and negation both are to be found in every judgement. From the standpoint of substance, the object is existent, eternal, universal and one, while from the standpoint of modes it is nonexistent, particular, ephemeral and many.

The Jainas have illustrated Syadvada by the anecdote of an elephant and six blind persons. These blind persons wanted to have an idea of the shape of the elephant. Touching the different parts of the body of the elephant with their hands, they mistook the particular parts of the elephant. Thus different persons touched different parts like ears, eyes, trunk, forehead, belly etc. and they formed their own conception about the shape of the elephant accordingly. One of them compared it to a fan, another to a pillar. For another blind person, it resembled a wall and so on. For every one of them, his own knowledge was absolute and correct, while that of others was wrong and contrary to facts. In the same way, all the philosophical schools embody one-sided truth. Thus, from its own standpoint, each philosophy is correct. But if it pretends to be the sole embodiment of absolute truth and dubs other philosophies false and fallacious, then it is thoroughly mistaken.

The Importance of the Word *Syat*

The Jainas insist that the world *syat* should necessarily be used before every *Naya*. The word *syat* prefixed to a judgement denotes that the truth of that judgement is confined to that particular context and that it may not hold good in other contexts. Therefore, according to the Jaina philosophers, the use of the word *syat* is imperative for rendering the judgement flawless and correct.

Criticism of *Syadvada*

Other Indian philosophical thinkers have bitterly criticised the Jaina theory of *Syadvada.* The reasons for criticism can be summarised as follows:

1. **The Buddhists and the Vedantins have regarded it as nothing more than a negative theory. They take *syad* in the sense of probability and they have based their criticism on it. The same thing cannot be present and absent in the same sense. Philosophers like Dharmakirti and Samkaracharya treat this theory as absolutely**

senseless. For Ramanuja it is impossible to roll into one, the contradictory qualities of existence and non-existence of something. It would be just bracketing light and darkness together. But the clarification given above exposes the ignorance of the Buddhists and Vedantin philosophers about *Syadvada.* According to the Jaina view, everything has more than one quality. It is many, non-existent and ephemeral from the standpoint of modes. A thing is existent from the viewpoints of its own substance and has a form, time and scope. Thus it admits no contradiction. A thing is regarded existent, non-existent and inexpressible not from one standpoint but from different standpoints. Thus, the Jaina philosophers retort that oblivious of this vital and fundamental fact and afraid of imaginary contradictions, foolish people regard the relative as the absolute and thus are led astray from truth.

2. The second objection, raised by Sankaracharya, nevertheless, points out a real defect of *Syadvada*. If everything, argues Sankara, is merely probable, then *Syadvada* cannot be an exception. In fact, the theory of *Anekantika* also hinges on *Ekantika*.

But mere togetherness does not mean coherence. In the absence of an absolute element, the diverse relative elements cannot be united by any means whatsoever. *Yasovijaya* asserts that *Anekantvada* is characterised by impartiality because it metes out the same treatment to all the different *nayas*. Just as a father does not and should not discriminate between his sons, so *Anekantavada* also does not differentiate between the various *Nayas*. But this equality tends to overlook the diversity and leads to dogmatism. According to Hem Chandra, all the philosophical schools, except the Jaina, are relative, biased and revel in criticising one another. Only the Jaina philosophy provides a welcome relief, as it is free from bias and treats the different *Nayas* alike.

As the absolute element is missing, this equality is reduced to mere accumulation. Really speaking, *Anekantavada* not only possesses relative truth, but also suffers from relative untruth. If all the theories are true only from a particular standpoint, how can the Jaina philosophy be an exception to this rule? It necessarily follows that the Jaina philosophical school must also contains, not absolute, but only relative truth. The Jainas refute the theory of reality as ineffable. But, as a matter of fact, the indescribable nature of the fourth *Naya* of *Syadvada* is but another name for what is regarded as ineffable. The Jainas themselves sometimes support absolutism. But they very conveniently forget it, when in all earnestness and with great fervour, they profound *Syadvada*.

The Jaina philosophy does not seek to transcend relativism and pluralism and so it does not recognise absolutism and monism. It does not distinguish between different relative judgements. By taking the absolute only as a combination of parts, the Jainas have blurred the conception of their *Kevala Jnana* also. They have thus made it ambiguous and indistinct. *Kevala Jnana* is otherworldly, absolute and immediate. But even then the Jainas refuse to differentiate between temporal and otherworldly (*Paramarthika*) knowledge. In fact, *Kevala Jnana* and *Syadvada* have become contradictory.

It is worth noting that some Jaina philosophers like Samantabhadra, Hem Chadnra and Siddhasena have drawn a distinction between temporal and otherworldly knowledge and have brought themselves nearer to Vedanta philosophy. In fact, without absolutism, the relativism of the Jainas is incomplete.

Jiva Tattva

The Jainas define Jiva or Atman as conscious substance. Atman in this world is known as Jiva. It has vital and physical, mental and sensuous powers. In its pure condition, Jiva has pure knowledge and vision i.e., Nirvikalpa and Savikalpa Jnana. But due to the effect of Karma, Jiva is yoked with five Bhavasatvas (body). Jiva with Pudgala or matter is termed as *sansari* or worldly. Jaina philosophy believes that causes change into real effects. So *bhavas* change into *dravya* and vice versa.

The Attributes of *Jivas*

Jiva is self-illuminated and illuminates other things also. It is eternal and pervades the whole body. It enjoys the fruits of actions and tends to go upwards. *Karma* enters into it due to eternal ignorance and binds it in fetters. The fettered Jiva is conscious, possessed of the qualities of flexibility and resilience, and assumes the form of the body it enters. The expansion of Jiva differs from that of inanimate objects. But Atman can enter into matter. Similarly, one Jiva can enter into another Jiva. Jiva has no form and is therefore not the object of eyes. Its existence is determined by self-experience. In the released state it attains right knowledge. Jiva has *pradesas*, which are also called *paryayas* or modes. Jiva is ever characterised by birth, destruction and eternity. Jiva is inherently possessed of infinite perception, infinite knowledge and infinite power. Their manifestation is blocked by the cloak of actions. In fact, the results of consciousness are the special attributes of Jiva. Knowledge is also of two kinds: attributed knowledge and knowledge without attributes i.e. *Kevala Jnana. Kevala Jnana* is pure and manifests itself after the annihilation of actions. The body no doubt, perishes, but not the soul or *bhava*, which, though assuming different forms-divine, human and hellish, is, nevertheless, eternal..

Proofs of the Existence of Soul

According to Jaina philosophers, the proofs for the existence of soul are also of two kinds, viz., direct and indirect. When we see the attributes or qualities of soul, we directly realise the existence of soul. The perception of attributes is tantamount to the perception of the substance. I feel that I am happy. This feeling enables me to have a direct realisation of the existence of soul. Similarly the experience of different attributes e.g., sorrow, memory, thought, doubt and knowledge leads to the direct realisation of the possessor of these attributes, i.e. the soul. In fact, the Jains reckon consciousness as the essence of the soul.

The following are the indirect proofs of the existence of the soul:

1. The body can be moved according to one's will. So there must be its mover, the soul.
2. The sense organs like eyes, ears etc. are the various instruments of knowledge. Without a co-ordinator, knowledge cannot be gathered through these sense organs. The soul is the required co-ordinator.
3. Besides material cause, an efficient cause is also required for the production of inanimate objects, e.g. a jar or a piece of cloth. The body also cannot come into existence without an efficient cause. The soul is the efficient cause of the existence of the body.

Bondage & Liberation

Feelings of greed and lust are the root cause of the bondage of *astrava,* and *pudgal* is the result of such thoughts. *Bhavastrava* is born before the entrance of *pudgals* into *jiva.* The bondage of *jiva* which follows it is known as Bhavabandha. Dravyastrava follows entrance of *pudgala* into *jiva.* The bondage, which involves *jiva* in it, is termed Dravya bandha. Astrava destroys the real form of *jiva* and consequently it is exposed to bondage. Apart from these two factors, there are other causes of the bandage of *jiva* like *karma*, falsehood, attachment and non-observance of the rules of penance. In the state of bondage, *jiva* and *pudgalas* enter into one another.

According to the Jaina philosophy, liberation is the escape of *Jiva* from matter. It is also its summum bonum. In Jaina philosophy, two kinds of liberation are conceived—*bhava moksa* and *dravya moksa.* Attachment and the like can be destroyed by obeying the laws or by meditation. Then *astrava* is destroyed by *sanvar* and *nirjana.* Thus, when it is freed of the matter and becomes supreme, like a superior spectator, it experiences freedom. This state is called *Bhava Moksa* or *Jiva Mukti.* This is the initial state of real liberation, in which the four destructible karmas—*Jnanavarniya*, *darsanavarniya*, *mohanaya* and *antaraya*—are destroyed. After this, the destruction of the four indestructible karmas—*ayu*, *nama*, *gotra*, *vedaniya*—leads to *dravya moksa.* At the same time, it is freed from the *aupasamika*, *kshayopasamika*, *audayika* and *bhavatva* state. Then, adopting vertical motion, it reaches the limits of the upper world. *Dharmastikaya* does not exist in the supernatural enlightened world. Thus, *Jiva* can neither proceed farther than this loka nor can return to the world. Consequently, it lives eternally in *Sidhashila.*

Thus, human freedom and liberation from bondage is one of the most important aspects of the Jaina philosophy which has its bearing on education during all times. No education can be fruitful if does not teach pupils to build character by developing non-attachment. Inspired by the Vedic traditions the Jainas try to build their own ways to get human beings redeemed from the bondage. The Jainas' approach to build character and to lead a sin-free life is perhaps one of the best approaches in the Indian philosophical schools.

The Ways to Attain *Moksa*

The Jainas have suggested different ways of obstructing the entry of *karma*. One of them is *panch mahavrata.* The *panch mahavrata* has great importance in stopping the entry of *karma* particles into the self by following the five vows—*ahimsa* (non-violence), *satya* (truthfulness), *asteya* (non-stealing), *brahmacharya* (celibacy) and *aparigraha* (non-covetousness)

(i) *Ahimsa*: This principle of the Jainas is based on the postulate that all beings are equal. In *ahimsa*, the mind, speech and action become permeated with non-violence. Ahimsa means abstention from annihilation of living beings. It forbids the killing of any beings, not just some beings. To follow this law is difficult for common house-hold people.

(ii) *Satya*: Satya or truth means (includes) the complete banishment of falsity. The ideal of truth to be observed is the truth accepted by and useful to all. Thus, the observance of *Satya Vrata* means not only staying at a distance from greed, fear and anger but also abstaining from decrying, ridiculing, and by using bad words etc.

(iii) *Asteya*: Asteya is the non-acceptance of material things from others without giving something in return. Ahimsa has intimate relation with *asteya*. Existence of life depends upon wealth, so looting of wealth amounts to killing of living beings. Thus thieving too is equally bad.

(iv) *Brahmacharya*: Sacrifice of or abstention from passion is called *brahmacharya* or celibacy. It implies the sacrifice of all actions, not merely of sensual pleasure. Complete sacrifice of all desires, whether mental or physical, fine or gross, worldly or supernatural, egoistic or altruistic is equally essential for observance of celibacy.

(v) *Aparigraha*: This means sacrifice of attachment to all objects of desire and implies sacrifice even of the objects of speech, touch, vision, taste and smell. Non-attachment to worldly objects is needed for liberation.

Dharma

The Jainas have enumerated ten *dharmas*, the obedience to which is a safeguard against karmas entering the soul. These ten *dharmas* are—forgiveness, sweetness, simplicity, cleanliness, truth, self-control, penance, sacrifice, indifference and celibacy. These *dharmas* are self explanatory and are a prerequisite to one's purification in life leading one to cultivate a sane life, free from vice and corrupt practices. The finest aspect of Jaina philosophy is their approach to the ten *dharmas*, which in fact are the ten main characteristics that crystallize a good human character. Leaving aside celibacy, which is not recommended for householders, all the other aspects placed under *dharma*, are

highly fruitful to build human conduct and are good for all times. This has a great bearing on education as character building is one of the main aspects of good education.

Nirjara Element

The destruction of *karma* particles which are the seeds of limitations is called *nirjara.* These particles are the ones already adhering to the self. The Jainas suggest sixty two methods that can prevent any further addition of *karma* particles but it is equally essential to destroy the old *karma* particles. That is why *nirjara* is needed. In order to arrive at this state, it is essential to sacrifice evil traits like attachment etc., and to have *nididhyasana*. This makes the mind flexible and pure and the Jiva can recognise the soul situated in its own body. Thereupon, the person becomes free from pain, and begins to experience self-realisation—the ultimate end of ethics, philosophy and religion.

Triratna or Three Jewels

Sanvar prevents any new influx or karma particles. Nirjara path to liberation is *triratna* or three jewels viz., right faith, right knowledge and right character.

1. *Right Faith*: According to Umaswami, right faith implies faith in real knowledge, i.e. in the essence of the Jaina preachings. Faith increases with meditation and it can be perfect only when complete knowledge has been obtained.
2. *Right Knowledge*: While in right faith the knowledge is merely of the essence of Jaina preachings, in right knowledge, there is specialized knowledge of the rudiments

of *Jiva* and *Ajiva*. It is beyond doubt and without defect. For this too, *karmas* must be destroyed. *Kevala Jnana* can come only after *karmas* have been destroyed.

3. *Right Character*: It includes the adoption of beneficial activities and the abandoning of harmful ones. This frees the *Jiva* from the *Karmas*. However, it requires the following observances:

    (i) Obedience to *panch mahavrata*.

    (ii) Carefulness in moving, talking, accepting favours and excreting urine etc.

    (iii) Practice of *Gupti* in mind, speech and religion.

    (iv) Conduct of ten *dharmas* viz., forgiveness, softness, simplicity, truth, cleanliness, self-control, penance, sacrifice, disenchantment and celibacy.

    (v) Feeling related to the real element in the *Jiva* and the world.

    (vi) Suffering pains of hunger, thirst, heat and cold.

    (vii) Practising equality, softness, munificence and good character.

The foregoing detailed description of the cause of bondage and the means for their removal must have made it quite clear that the Jaina philosophers had a great insight into the field of human experience. It is also true consequently that to a great extent Jaina philosophy has made a significant contribution to Indian ethics. The triratna are certainly prerequisites to character building which is the need of the hour and one of the major requirements of education these days besides providing knowledge to human beings. In that respect Jainas are unparalleled and need to be adhered to.

Questions

1. What do you understand by the categories of knowledge according to the Jainas? In what way can this sort of knowledge be helpful to you as a student of education?
2. Define *Syadvada* and its importance in Jaina philosophy? How do Buddhists and Vedantins react to the Jaina theory of *Syadvada*? Does *Syadvada* have any impact on educating a person in your view?
3. Is it possible to attain freedom by the soul (Jiva) in ways suggested by the Jainas? Which of them are easily applicable by a worldly human being? Which of them would you as a teacher recommend most to your students in life?
4. How far are the ten *Dharmas* suggested by the Jains useful to a human being to lead a happy and prosperous life in the modern times? Do they have any bearing on building human conduct? Comment briefly!
5. Comment on Jains' views on destroying *Karma* by leading a Nirjara path to attain complete freedom. How far can these ways be practised by an ordinary human being? To what extent would it be possible for you as a teacher to help your students practise some of those ways to make them free from vice and live happily?

Chapter Six

The Philosophy of Buddha

Historical Perspective

The founder of the Buddhist philosophy Siddhartha Gautama was born in 563 B.C., at Lumbini, in Kapilvastu, in Uttar Pradesh. His mother, Mayadevi, died seven days after his birth. He was brought up by his aunt, Gautami. From his childhood Siddhartha showed a meditative bent of mind. At the age of sixteen he was married to Yashodhara—a Kshatriya princess. She bore him a son who was given the name Rahul. At the age of twenty nine, Gautam renounced his home to find a solution to the world's perpetual sorrows of death, sickness and suffering. He went to the forest of Urvela where he meditated for six years, but he was not contended. He then went to Buddha Gaya and meditated under a Pipal tree. It was here that he attained enlightment and came to be known as Buddha. He then went to a long journey to spread the message of the great truths. The number of his followers started to increase, and so he collected a group of five hundred to make a sect which rigorously adhered to the rules he laid down for its conduct. In 483 B.C., at a place called Kushinara, Gautama Buddha attained the condition of *mahaparinirvana* at the age of 80.

Gautama's three main followers, Upali, Anand and Mahakashyap remembered his teachings and undertook to communicate them to his other followers. Later on, it was at the meeting of the Third Buddha assembly under the guidance of Ashoka, which took place in 247 B.C. at Pataliputra, that the teachings of Buddha were collected together. His disciples divided these teachings into three parts called the *Vinay Pitaka*, the *Sutta Pitaka* and *Abhidhamma Pitaka*, which form the basic texts of the Buddhist literature. But the sects established by Buddha chose to interpret his teachings according to their own whims which led to the division of the Buddhist sect into two groups—called the Mahayana and the Hinayana.

Main Characteristics

The school of Indian philosophy that has been most popular among the masses outside India is the philosophy of Buddha. Buddha's philosophy essentially popularised *upanishadic* thought, though in a different form. To understand this change of form, one must understand the social conditions prevailing in that period. It is known from the Tripitaka books that in Buddha's time and before him, discussions on self, world, other world, sins and liberation etc. were very common. Politically, the country was divided into a number of small states whose inhabitants used different languages. The philosophical systems had not till then assumed systematic forms. The *Vedas* were considered as sacred in the spiritual field. In the moral field, reasoning was given more importance than practice. Ethics was based on religion and religion depended on God. Hence the importance of human efforts and the sense of responsibility gradually started disappearing. Everywhere superstition, useless discussion and irresponsible conduct became common. Gautama revolted against these tendencies and presented a rational religion, practical ethics and simple principles of life that follow here under.

1. Aversion of Discussion

Though Buddha always tried to explain his principles intellectually, he usually avoided long discussions. In this sense he was an anti-intellectualist. Towards superstition he had the approach of a modern scientist. Buddha's religion and ethics are based on self-reliance. The teachings of Buddha are grounded more in deep analysis and wide experience than in intellectual discussion. The aim of Gautama was not intellectual discussion on philosophical concepts, but liberation from miseries. Whether the body is different or non-different from the self, whether the self is immortal or mortal, whether the world is finite or infinite, eternal or ephemeral, these are philosophical questions about which he kept silent. Intellectual discussions on these philosophical topics may have their own merit, but they hardly help in the achievement of liberation from misery.

Buddha considered it useless to search for an answer to the ten philosophical questions. In the Pali literature of the Buddhist religion, these questions have been called, 'Avyaktani'. Sometimes their number was given as even more than ten. These questions were as follows:

(i) Is the world eternal?

(ii) Is it non-eternal?

(iii) Is it finite?

(iv) Is it infinite?

(v) Are the body and the self the same?

(vi) Is the self different from body?

(vii) Does the Tathagat take birth again after death?

(viii) Does he not take birth again after death?

(ix) Are there re-birth and also no re-birth?

(x) Are the concepts of re-birth and no rebirth false?

From the practical standpoint the answers to these questions are useless and from the philosophical standpoint no final solution can be secured. Hence Buddha rejected them all.

2. Pessimism

Another important characteristic of Buddha's philosophy is pessimism. Buddha considered the world as full of misery, so it was man's duty to obtain liberation from the painful world. He suggested remedies for these miseries and indicated the path of liberation. Thus, Buddha's philosophy, though beings with pessimism, culminates in optimism.

3. Realism

Buddha vehemently criticized blind faith in the traditional scripture like the *Vedas* etc. He did not admit the existence of God as he believed in the doctrine of *karma*. He emphasized the importance of real experiences of life, and recommended making earnest efforts to attain liberation.

4. Pragmatism

Buddha's teachings are most pragmatic. It is due to their pragmatic importance that Buddha has discussed the four great truths and said, "It is by such a discussion that one can get again some gain; it is these which are closely related to the basic principles of religion. It is through the detachment and destruction of passions that the miseries may end and mental peace, knowledge, wisdom and *nirvana* may be attained".

Four Noble Truths

Once during a walk outside his palace, Siddhartha Gautama came upon an old person, a sick man, a corpse and a hermit. He was so profoundly stirred by these sights that he renounced his kingly pleasures and left home in search of truth. Ultimately he found the cause of suffering and the means of removing it. Finally he attained enlightenment. The knowledge realised by him is comprehended in four noble truths. These Noble Truths are as follows:

1. There is Suffering

Observing human suffering, the Buddha came to the conclusion that human life was painful. This concept is found in a number of his statements, like:

"There is pain with birth, destruction too is painful. Separation from the pleasant is also painful. Conjunction with the undesired is painful and passions which remain unsatiated and unfulfilled are painful. In brief, *Panchaskandha* springing from attachment is painful." In this way, contrary to *Carvaka*, the Buddha looks upon the momentary things of the world as painful and preaches means of escaping from suffering.

2. There is a Cause to the Suffering

According to the Buddha, the second Noble Truth pertains to the causes of suffering. Desire, the motivating force sustaining the cycle of birth and death, is the fundamental cause of sorrow. This desire is of three types—(1) Sex desire for sensual pleasure; (2) Life desire for enjoyment of life; and (3) Wealth desire for worldly wealth. All sorrows arise from attachment which itself is the result of ignorance.

3. There is Cessation of Suffering

The third Noble Truth, according to the Buddha, is in respect of the destruction of pain. In it, passion, desire and love of life are completely destroyed. Desires are to be completely sacrificed and our total separation from them is required to lead a peaceful life. The subject of this Noble Truth is the elimination of sorrow. *Nirvana* is the destruction of passion, doubt and sensual pleasure by contemplation on Nothing or *Sunya*. "Dig out the roots of desire so that it may not crush you time and again".

4. Path of Liberation

The fourth Noble Truth is the path to cessation of sorrow. The Buddha not only identified the causes of sorrow but also sent a current of hope in a world of pessimism by showing the path to remove those causes. This path is eightfold. Pursuing this path, the Buddha attained the stage of absolute liberation, which others can also achieve if they pursue it. Actually, this is the essence of Buddhist religion and the four Noble Truths are the foundation stone of Buddhist philosophy. They also reflect the entire circle of Gautama's spiritual life which had its origin in consciousness of suffering and the discovery of means of escape from suffering. Thus, Gautama's spiritualism is based on solid realism.

Nirvana

The ultimate end of Buddha's philosophy is *nirvana* which literally means 'extinguished'. Some people interpret it to mean the end of life. This idea, however, is wrong. Had it been so, the Buddha would not have attained *nirvana* before his death. It is equally incorrect to interpret the Buddha's silence to mean that the person who achieves *nirvana* has no existence after death. *Nirvana* means the extinction of the fires of passions. In it, the fires of avarice, jealousy, anger and doubt are extinguished and impurities of the mind like sexual, ignorant and affective tendencies come to an end. It affects the end of the cycle of rebirth. **The Nirvana is said to be a state of equanimity in which passions and the sorrows are completely becalmed. Nirvana can be attained in this life. A rational and social life is not precluded from it. The Buddha's own life exemplifies this. Nirvana does not imply abstention from action but from the attachment, repulsion and labour conjoined to action. In the state of nirvana, the body does not cease to exist but the craving is destroyed. It is similar to 'liberation while living', a conception of the Upanishads. But there is no rebirth after Nirvana.**

In *nirvana*, the individual's ego is destroyed because its substratum, pain and longing etc, has been completely eliminated. *Nirvana* in every conceivable aspect is a state of unrestricted calm. A free person has perfect impassion, pure peace, perfect self-control, calm mind, calm word and calm actions.

Result of Nirvana

With *nirvana* the causes for birth come to an end and the probability or rebirth and pain after death is excluded. The person who has achieved *nirvana* spends a life of perfect knowledge and becomes calm till death. It can only be said that in *nirvana* man is delivered from all pain.

Buddha's Middle Path

From the philosophical and moral point of view, the Buddha has advocated a middle path which means to avoid the two extremes. On the one hand, there are the pleasure of sensual objects, interest in passions and undirected pleasure seeking life should be avoided. On the other hand, there is the habit of suppressing the self. It is painful and worth discarding. Thus, the Buddha discovered a middle path in between these two extremes. It guides man towards peace and insight, supreme wisdom and *nirvana*. It can be attained through the noble eightfold path.

Eightfold Path

The noble eightfold path of the Buddha is as follows:

1. Right Vision

The first means in the Buddha's eightfold path is right vision. Ignorance generates a wrong view of the relation between the world and self. Man mistakes a transient painful and unspiritual object for a permanent, blissful and spiritual one. The abandoning of this view and understanding the real nature of objects is said to be the right vision.

2. Right Resolve

The second way is right resolve. The determination to root out thoughts which entertain ill will and a desire to do harm to others or contemplate attachment to sensual pleasure is the right resolve. Right volition should accompany right vision. Right volition includes sacrifice, benevolence and sympathy.

3. Right Speech

The third way is right speech. As a first step, man should control his speech by right resolve. Right speech means avoidance of false or unlikeable speech or criticism. Every man should avoid bad speech and adopt a good one. One word which can calm the mind is better than hundreds of meaningless words.

4. Right Conduct

The fourth means is proper conduct, which means refraining from activities like destruction of life, theft, sexuality, falsifying, excessive eating, social recreations, pursuit of artificial means of beauty, jewellery, comfortable beds and gold, etc. All these laws apply to the hermits. But married people need obey only five laws. For ordinary people there are a number of other laws. Parents should protect their children from evil traits and cultivate good qualities in them. The children should serve their aged parents; the students should study, respect their teachers, obey them and fulfil their needs; the teachers should behave lovingly towards them and perfect them in the arts and sciences and cultivate good habits in them. The husband should respect his wife, be faithful to her and look after her welfare; the wife should behave lovingly towards her husband, manage the home efficiently, be hospitable to all guests and maintain marital fidelity.

5. Right Means of Livelihood

Right livelihood means earning one's bread by the right means. Without it, right activity cannot be fully practised. According to the Buddha, one should not trade in weapons, animals, meat, wine, etc. No person should earn money by unfair and bad means like pressure, fraud, bribe and dacoity etc.

6. Right Effort

Along with obedience to laws, it is also necessary to stop bad impressions and bad feelings. Such efforts are known as right efforts, which include self-control, negation of sensuality, stopping bad thoughts, cultivating good thoughts and concentrating the mind upon universal welfare. The Buddha advocates the following modes to restrict bad thoughts.

7. Right Mindfulness

Right mindfulness means the retention of the body, the conscience, and the mind in their real form. Bad thoughts occupy the mind only when their real form is forgotten. When actions take place according to bad thoughts, pain has to be suffered. Right mindfulness includes the remembering of the impurities of the body, pleasure, nature of pain, hatred and doubtful mind. Right mindfulness destroys attachment and releases one from pain.

Gautama, the Buddha, described right mindfulness meticulously. He preached that body should be treated as constituted of earth, water, fire and air. It is filled with deplorable things like bones, skin, intestines, spleen, urine etc. The remembering of these truths makes one forget love and attachment for one's own and another's body. Due to this, the attachment to other evil tendencies is also destroyed. In this way, man avoids worldly attachment.

8. Right Concentration

By pursuing the seven laws stated above, man's tendencies of the *citta* or mind are pacified and he becomes capable of entering right concentration. Before *Nirvana* is attained, right concentration has the following four stages

(i) In the first stage, the four Noble Truths are meditated upon with a calm mind. Pure and detached thought creates unique happiness.

(ii) In the second stage, efforts like meditations are suppressed and reasoning becomes unnecessary. Doubts are removed and faith in Noble Truths increases. Hence intuition replaces thought. Profound contemplation results in peace and evenness in the mind. At the same time, bliss also is experienced.

(iii) The third stage is one of indifference. Here the endeavour is to remove happiness and introduce indifference in the mind. In this stage, the mind is in equilibrium, but one becomes indifferent to the happiness of concentration.

(iv) The condition of absolute peace is the fourth stage in which pleasure and pain are destroyed and the tendencies of the mind are negated. It is a stage of perfect peace, perfect indifference, and perfect negation. In it, pain is completely destroyed and *nirvana* attained.

Doctrine of Karma

The doctrine of *karma* in Buddhist philosophy is based upon the doctrine of dependent origination. Accordingly the present life of man is the result of his past life and the future depends upon the present. According to the Buddhist philosophy, "Because of their *Karmas*, men are not similar, but some are long-living, some short-living, some healthy and some un-healthy etc." ***According to the doctrine of Karma, every man is responsible for his actions. The actions must bear fruit. The future of every individual depends on***

his present actions. According to the doctrine of karma, the fruits of the action are according to the character of the actor. If a bad man commits a sin, he will have to suffer for it in hell. But if a good man by chance commits the same, he will get rid of it after suffering a little in this very life. It is like this, if a man puts some salt in a small cup of water, the water will become salty and not worthy of drinking; but if the same amount of salt is thrown in the water of the Ganges, it will have no marked effect.

When the doctrine of *Karma* becomes all-powerful, human freedom disappears. If everything is predetermined according to *Karmas*, how can an individual effect any change in it? Gautama the Buddha has not given any clear answer to the question of human freedom *vis-a-vis* the doctrine of *Karma*. But he has accepted the possibility of overcoming the entire law of *karma* and the actuality of free actions of *karma* is not mechanical. As a matter of fact, if the doctrine of *karma* is mechanical then there is hardly any place for religion and ethics in human life. **The doctrine of karma shows an order in the field of spiritual development as well as in that of terrestrial process. It does not lessen the importance of effort and responsibility. The philosophy of the Buddha is against absolute determinism as well as against absolute indeterminism. One of the important aspects of the doctrine of karma suggested by the Buddhists is the training of mind to build human character, which is also an important aspect of education. All kinds of educational approaches stress on building human character so that each human being could live peacefully and let others also lead a peaceful life. In that respect, the Buddhist approach is outstanding and highly educative.**

Theory of No-soul

The Buddha does not believe in any permanent soul. Consciousness is an eternal process resulting from the relation of antecedent and subsequent between different movements. But there is no unchanging soul behind this process. Hence logically there is no place for rebirth in Buddhist philosophy. After death the predispositions of the *jiva* remain. These predispositions are according to his *Karma* and it is because of that, that a link between one birth and another is maintained. This predisposition is expressed in the last thought of a dying person. Along with this power of *Karma*, attachment or clinging (*Upadan*) is also required. This clinging is the power which causes the new birth according to old *karmas*. Without it the *karmas* have no power. After the attainment of liberation, attachment and clinging are annihilated. It results in the negation of rebirth. There is no similarity between the past and the present individual except that the new is according to the *Karmas* of the old. Sometimes even consciousness has been admitted as the remaining after death. "Whatever we are or whatever we think is the result of it. Consciousness has been rightly conceived as the essence of our soul." After the attainment of *nirvana*, one is liberated both from consciousness and from actions.

The theory of no-soul also follows from the doctrine of dependent origination. There is no invisible, permanent substance besides the flow of consciousness. As the body is destroyed, the five *skandhas* disappear into five elements (*Pancha Bhutas*) and nothing remains besides the *Upadan* or Karma. This principle is known as the theory of no-soul in the Buddha's philosophy.

The Buddha has explained the continuity of life with the example of the flame of a lamp. There is cause and effect relation between antecedent and subsequent states of life. Life is a systematic and continuous process through different states. Like the flame of a lamp, it is changing every moment. The flame of a lamp at every moment depends on the state preceding it and the subsequent state is the result of the present state. Hence life is homogeneous. The flame of a lamp at every moment depends on the conditions prevailing at that time, but in spite of the difference in different flames, they appear to be the same due to continuity. The Buddha believes in rebirth and the principle of *karma*. He, however, does not believe in rebirth in the sense that a soul enters in a different body after leaving one body, but rebirth means that another birth follows every birth just as a lamp can be lighted by another lamp and yet the lights of both cannot be identified. Similarly in spite of cause and effect relation between the two births is different.

Doctrine of Momentariness

The Buddha holds that, "All the existing things have been created due to some cause. All these things are non-eternal in every way." "Whatever appears to be eternal and permanent is also perishable. Whatever appears to be great has also its decline. Where there is union there is also separation. Where there is birth there is also death." "Five things are absolutely inevitable; whoever can be old, he must become old; whoever can be ill, he must fall ill; whoever is subordinate to death, he must die; whatever is perishable, its destruction is imperative, and whatever is non-eternal, it must go." These rules cannot be violated by any worldly or divine power. This view is a middle way between the principles of absolute existence and absolute *nihilism*.

This doctrine of impermanence (*Anityavad*) of the Buddha was given the form of the doctrine of momentariness by his

disciples. As a matter of fact, the doctrine of momentariness follows from the principles of dependent origination. Whatever is born will also be destroyed and whatever may be destroyed cannot think to be permanent. Hence everything is momentary.

Let teachers of education keep in mind the doctrine of momentariness to remind their pupils that nothing is permanent in this world therefore all must exert to do good for fellow beings and should not indulge in avarice, greed and lustful activities so that they could be free from pain and sufferings. In this respect Buddha's precepts are unparalleled and highly educative to the common man who is constantly keeping busy in the base activities and low thinking which are conducive to develop a good conduct. Therefore, all this is highly related to the realm of education.

Questions

1. How far do Buddha's four noble truths have any bearing on modern education practices? Discuss critically.
2. Discuss Buddha's eightfold path briefly and list their importance in human life.
3. Buddha's theory of Karma does not leave any room for human freedom. Still he suggests that a human has freedom and can divert his/her efforts to the right direction if he/she adopts the eightfold path. Discuss how a man can retain his freedom and lead a sane life if he so desires in the light of Buddha's eight-fold path.
4. Compare Buddha's and Jains' approaches in defining soul. On what grounds does Buddha reject the existence of a soul? How far as a student of educational philosophy do you agree with the Buddhist approach of 'no-soul'?

Chapter Seven

Nyaya Philosophy

Historical Perspective

The *Nyaya* philosophy represents the fines development of logic in the Indian philosophical tradition. *Nyaya Sutra*, the basic text of this philosophy, was composed by Gautama. Initially it was meant to dispose of the arguments of the supporters of the Buddhist sect, but it aimed at finding a way out of human suffering. The most refined expression of it is to be found in *Nyaya Suchi Nibandha* written by Vachaspati. It is the only extant text on *Nyaya* philosophy. Of the many elaborate treatises written on this text, the most famous is the treatise of Vatsyayan written in the second century A.D. In the twelfth century, a school of thought known as neo-*Nyaya* philosphy came into existence due to the efforts of Gangesh Upadhyaya of Mithila. As a result, all previous texts came to be considered ancient. The latest treatise differed from the earlier philosophy as it concentrated on the intricacies of logic, while its predecessors were simply concerned with liberation. Hence *Nyaya* philosophy as it provides the techniques of logical thinking, certainly retains importance in Indian Philosophy

Epistemology

Nyaya has specialised in the field of logic and epistemology. Knowledge has been explained as the manifestation of objects. Knowledge enlightens the objects like a lamp. Knowledge has two distinctions—valid (*prama*) and invalid (*aprama*). According to *Nyaya*, valid knowledge is definite as real knowledge and it consists of knowing the object as it is. For example, to know a snake as a snake, and a bowl as a bowl is valid knowledge. Valid knowledge has four distinctive sources viz., perception, inference, comparison and testimony. Knowledge that arises from sources other than these is called invalid or *aprama* knowledge.

Thus, the theory of knowledge is an important contribution of the *Nyaya* philosophers and is highly useful when applied to the field of education. Education is that dimension which awakens one's unexplored areas of mind and knowledge. If the knowledge received by the pupil or even by the teacher is not valid it cannot be fruitful and can't help him/her to get awakened to the realities of life which are interwoven by so many confusing issues in life. Hence *Nyaya* epistemology is worth keeping in mind to receive things in their true form.

Perception

According to Gautama, perception is undisputed knowledge. It arises out of the proximity of the object with the sense organ. It is distinct and unrelated to any name. According to this view, perception is that form of knowledge which results from the contact or nearness between the object and the sense organs, and this is real knowledge. For example, when any object is so near to the eye that one has no doubt whatsoever as to its being real, then it is perceptual knowledge. If a distinct object appears to be a human being and if there are some doubts about this knowledge, then in spite of the actual contact between the sense organs and the object, that knowledge is not perceptual knowledge. In the same way, knowledge of the rope as the snake is not perceptual knowledge even though it is not attended by any doubt. Hence, illusory knowledge cannot be considered to be perceptual. The *Nyaya* philosophers have recognised six kinds of proximity—*samyog, samyak samavaya, samyut samaveta, samavaya, samaveta samavaya* and *visesana visesya bhava.* **This analysis of perception does not take into account the extraordinary and intuitive perceptions because there can be no knowledge of them without contact with senses. Knowledge of pleasure and pain, etc., occurs without real contact with the sense organs. In this way, the general characteristic of perception is not contact with the senses but rather immediate cognition.** Perceptual knowledge of an object occurs only when there is cognition of it. It means that in perception, knowledge occurs without any past experience or inference. In this way, some *Nyaya* philosophers have given the name of perception (*pratiti*) to cognition, implying that perception is that knowledge which is not the result of any other knowledge.

Inference

The second source of valid knowledge according to *Nyaya* philosophy is inference. Inference is the means to *anumana*. It is past or indirect (*paroksa*) knowledge and takes place through the medium of some mark which is called the *hetu*. *Anumana* literally means that knowledge which follows some other knowledge. The basis of inference is the relation of invariable concomitance. The invariable relation between the *hetu* and the *sadhya* is called concomitance or *vyapti*. The knowledge of the qualities of the *paksa* through the *hetu* is called *paramarsa* or judgement.

Hence, inference or *Anumana* is said to be the knowledge gained through judgement, or in other words, the knowledge of the presence of the *sadhya* in the *paksa* through the *linga*, which is a quality of *paksa* and is invariably related by concomitance. For example, there is fire on the hill, because there is smoke on the hill, and where there is smoke there is fire. Here, there is the relation or invariable concomitance between smoke and fire. For this reason the presence of fire on the hill is inferred by the presence of the smoke on the hill because of concomitance. It has been observed on previous occasions that fire is invariably present where there is smoke.

Constituents of Inference

In an inference there are three items put in at least three sentences. These three constituents of inference are respectively called *paksa*, *sadhya* and *hetu*. They are similar to the three items—minor, major and middle—of the syllogism of western logic. *Paksa* is that part of the inference about which there is inference. *Sadhya* denotes that which is proved of the *paksa. Hetu* establishes that there is relation between the *Sadhya* and the *paksa*. For this reason, *hetu* is also known as the means. To illustrate by means of an example, in the above inference of fire on the hill, smoke is the means of inference. It is the *linga* or *hetu* or sign, the observation of which leads to the inference of the fire. This inference is based upon the invariable concomitance between fire and smoke. In this way, the inference of fire from smoke involves three steps:

1. There is smoke on the hill.
2. There is variable concomitance between smoke and the fire (of which we are already aware).
3. There is fire on the hill

Here the hill is the *paksa* because it is in its relation that the inference is being made. Fire is the *sadhya* because it is fire which is being proved of the *paksa* (hills), and smoke is the *linga*. In this way from the standpoint of thought process, the first step in this inference is knowledge of *paksa* with the *hetu*, the second is the knowledge of the *vypati* between *paksa* and *sadhya* and finally, the judgement about the relation of the *sadhya* with the *paksa*. This inference will be stated in the following manner.

There is fire on the hillside.

Because there is smoke on the hillside.

Where there is smoke there is fire.

It would be evident from the foregoing description of *Nyaya* that it is epistemological. Nyaya philosophy is second to no other system of Indian philosophy. After going through their detailed and subtle exposition of this subject, it cannot be said that logic has not been adequately developed in the Indian philosophy.

The Concept of God

God is the creator, sustainer and destroyer of the universe. He is the efficient, not the material, cause of the universe. He directs the activities of living souls, just as an intelligent and benevolent person inspires the son to act according to his intelligence, capability and qualities. So also, God inspires living beings to act according to the tendencies acquired by them in the past and to win rewards appropriate to their actions. It is He who determines the pains and pleasure of the *jivas*, provides their merits and rewards in view of their actions. He creates the universe from eternal entities such as atoms, space, time, ether, mind and souls which live with Him. It is because of His desire that the universe remains in its state of stability. In this way, it is He who also sustains the universe. He employs His powers or destruction when it becomes imperative that the universe should be destroyed.

Substances such as space, and time, have the same relation to God as the body has to the soul. Consequently they do not limit Him. He is all powerful unlike man whose power is limited by his virtues and sins. He has real knowledge of all objects and occurrences. He is, therefore, omniscient. He is the substratum in which knowledge exists. He is Himself knowledge. In Him are the six perfections. He is majestic, almighty, all glorious, infinitely beautiful and has infinite knowledge possessing perfect freedom from attachment.

Proofs of the Existence of God

The *Nyaya* philosophers have put forward many proofs of the existence of God. Some of them are:

1. *God is the creator of the organic objects of the universe*: There are two kinds of objects in the universe—organic and inorganic. The atoms of space, time, ether, soul, mind, earth, water, fire and air are perfect and eternal. Hence, there cannot be any question of their creator. But objects other than these are neither atomic nor all-pervading (*vibhu*). Hence, they must necessarily have some cause. Without the guidance and direction by an intelligent agent, their material cause cannot give them the form or shape they are possessing. This agent must possess the knowledge, the desire to attain the objective, and the power to make an effort. He must also be omniscient

otherwise he cannot have knowledge of such microscopic existence as the atoms. All these qualities are to be found only in a god. This proves the existence of God as the creator of the universe.

2. *God is the cause of differences in fortune and the ruler of past tendencies*: In this world, the fortune of everyone is different. One is born in a rich family and another in the poor. Some do not get a full meal even after a great labour while others have everything at their beck and call. Some are intelligent and others foolish. *Nyayaikas* believe that this difference is due to their past *adrsta.* This entity, called *adrsta*, is a result of merits and demerits developing from good or bad actions of the past. Good actions create merit in our souls and bad actions create demerit. According to this *adrsta*, the individual is the recipient of pleasure and pain in this as well as in the subsequent lives. But *adrsta* is unintelligent and hence it cannot itself create correlation in the past actions and their results. For this an intelligent director and guide is needed. The *Jivatma* cannot be the guide of an *adrsta*, because it does not have any knowledge of its past tendencies. Thus, according to the *Nyayaikas*, only God who is immortal, all powerful and omniscient, can be the guide of past tendencies.
3. *God is the cause of the validity of religious text*: The *Vedas* are valid and authoritative, and hence their creator, God, is also authoritative. Just as a science can be declared valid after testing even only a part of it, similarly the *Vedas* including their supernatural dictum may be accepted as valid after testing the validity about the worldly things.

The validity of the *Vedas* depends upon their author. The author of the *Vedas* cannot be a *Jiva* since he cannot be cognizant of their supernatural and extra-sensory subjects. The author of the *Vedas* can only be one who has perceptual and actual knowledge of the past, the present and the future, the atoms and cosmos, and of sensible and extra-sensory objects. For this reason, the creator of the *Vedas* is God and their validity emanates from Him.

4. *Divine utterances also prove the existence of God*: The fourth proof about the existence of God comes from *srti*, the *Vedic* scriptures. The existence of God has been accepted by the *Vedas,* the *Upanishads* and the *Gita.* The existence of God can be proved by experience and not by logic. For this reason, those individuals who do not have personal experience should depend upon *Srti* or divine utterances. According to Kusumanjali, *Srti* is evidence enough to prove the existence of God.

Criticism

Some arguments have been given against the proofs for the existence of God which *Nyayaikas* have put forward. They have been answered by the *Nyaya* philosophers. The major among them are:

1. In connection with the foregoing third and fourth proofs for the existence of God, it may be objected that they are interdependent, and consequently suffer from the fallacy of circular argument. But Sarva Darsana holds that their interdependence is not circular. It could be circular only if the two subjects had been interdependent from the same

point of view. In this particular case, from the viewpoint of existence, the *Vedas* are dependent upon God because God is their author, while from the viewpoint of human knowledge God is dependent upon the *Vedas* because it is through the *Vedas* that human beings get to know God.

2. The second objection in the *Nyaya* conception of God is that if God is the creator of this universe, he must possess a body, because without a body no activity can be indulged in. The *Nyayaikas* answer this by saying that the existence of God is either proved or disproved by the *Srti*. If it is proved then such an objection is useless.
3. The third objection of the *Nyaya* conception of God is concerned with the purpose which God has in creating the universe. It is argued that God can have no purpose of his own in creating the universe because He is perfect. He could not be doing it for others because one who works for the good of others cannot be wise. If creating the universe is simply because of benevolence, then there should not have been so many unhappy individuals in this world. Hence, God cannot be considered a creator of this world. The *Nyayaikas* provide a befitting answer to it and say that **God has created this world out of compassion** and it is only natural that there should be pain and pleasure in the world, because the *jivatmas* are attended by their respective *adrsta*. Just as mind is not the slave of the body though it helps it in the achievement of its object, in much the same way, the universe does not make the God dependent upon His creation but helps Him in the realisation of His objective.

Questions

1. Describe how *Nyaya* philosophy is different from other Indian philosophies and its importance to a student of philosophy?
2. Describe briefly *Nyaya*'s epistemological approach to reach the right knowledge. How far is it useful in the context of education to a student in his/her future life?
3. The proofs of God's existence provided by the *Nyaya* philosophers don't seem to be different from that of the Jain philosophers. Reflect upon their approaches critically and bring out similarities and differences, if any.
4. One of the best approaches of *Nyaya* philosophers is their logical approach to problem solving. How far could *Nyaya*'s approach be helpful to you to solve questions of a difficult nature in your life if you encounter them? Does this kind of approach have any bearing on education? Examine critically.

Chapter Eight

The Advaita Vedant Philosophy

Historical Perspective

Jaimini's philosophy is known as *Purva Mimamsa* and Vedanta philosophy is known as *Uttar Mimamsa.* Vedanta implies the philosophy of the *Upanishads* as they are the basic writings of Vedanta philosophy. Sankaracharya was born in 788 A.D., and lived till 820 A.D. He was the disciple of Govindpada. Samkaracharya's primary aim in writing the treatise on the Brahmasutra was to rejuvenate Vedic religion and to denounce the Buddhists and other atheistic sects. Although there is some difference of opinion about the time in which Sankaracharya lived, most scholars are inclined to believe that it was around the end of the eighth century.

It is said that Sankaracharya began his life as a worshipper of the Goddess Sakti but later he became a Vaishnava, and still later renounced the world and became a *sanyasi.* It is because of this that his writings include prayers to Shakti and Vishnu. In fact, although Sankaracharya believed in a single reality, Brahma, at the transcendental level, he accepted the importance of religion. Many different texts are attributed to Sankaracharya, but it is difficult to determine the genuine ones. Of the more famous works are his treatises written on the *Brahmasutra, Gita,* ten *Upanishads* and *Mandukya Karika.*

The Advaita or Non-dualism of Sankaracharya is a unique Indian contribution to the entire philosophical world. Even before Sankaracharya and also after him, many philosophical systems were developed in India which specialized in the different spheres of philosophy, but from the spiritual standpoint, the Advaita philosophy holds an unrivalled position. Thus, whether we agree or not with the Advaita philosophy, it makes a profound impression by its deep insight and consistent logic.

Epistemology

According to Sankaracharya, the so-called means of knowledge do not give us real knowledge. They only remove ignorance being based on the distinction between subject and object. Real knowledge is beyond these. The means of knowledge work only in the field of ignorance. Knowledge requires no means, nor any proofs, since it is self-illumined and self-proved. But just as the disappearance of the illusion of snake leads to the real knowledge of the rope, similarly, the very removal of ignorance leads to knowledge. As a matter of fact, there is no sharp line dividing the removal of ignorance and the beginning of knowledge. Knowledge is the disappearance of ignorance. Hence, knowledge of the self and of the Brahman occupies a prominent place in Advaita philosophy, while epistemology has been given a subordinate place. Advaita philosophy denies the reality of the truth of name and form as presented by the sense organs. So it cannot rely upon the knowledge acquired through senses. However, such knowledge may be helpful in every-day life. Thus, according to Sankaracharya, all means of knowledge and all knowledge acquired through them are unreal from the transcendental standpoint. But one cannot deny their importance from the practical standpoint.

In Vedanta, *prama* means the valid knowledge which is undisputed. *Prama* does not include knowledge through memory. It is that knowledge only which has never been attained before. It may be pointed out here that in perception, the object is known only by linking the present perception the perception of the moments already passed. But according to Vedanta, there is only one state of the mind in so far as there is only one object of perception. Hence there is no question of the antecedent and subsequent.

According to Vedanta, there are three *pramanas*, viz., perception (*Pratyksa*), inference (*Tarka*) and scripture (*Srti*):

1. Perception

The identity of the subject and object consciousness by *citta* adopting the form of the external object is perception. Hence according to Advaita, in perception, the subject and the object become identical. The subject and the object remain separate due to ignorance. By the direct contact of the *anntahkarana* with the object through the senses, it takes the form of the object and shines in that particular form illumined by the self due to the removal of the ignorance. This definition of perception, in spite of its being very much imperfect from the scientific standpoint, according to Advaita clarifies the fact that it is the same consciousness that exists both in the subject and the object, which appear different only on account of ignorance.

2. *Tarka* or Inference

Inference is the knowledge which results from the past impressions. It is based upon the awareness of between two terms. The awareness of concomitance leaves the impressions on the *citta* and when these impressions are awakened by perceiving that object again, the result is inference. For example, after being aware of the relation between fire and smoke, one can infer about the existence of fire. Hence Vedanta admits only concomitance in presence. It does not admit other types of concomitances admitted by *Nyaya* philosophy. Against *Nyaya* philosophy, Sankaracharya admits only three premises of an inference. These are:

1. *Pratijna*—Everything different from Brahman is unreal.
2. *Hetu*—Because all things are different from Brahman.
3. *Udaharana*—So all things are unreal as seeing of silver in nacre.

3. Srti or Scripture

In Advaita, *Agama* or *Veda* has been admitted as an independent testimony and source of knowledge. The *Vedas* are impersonal and eternal, though they are not such in so far as they are written scriptures. According to *Advaita* philosophy, the *Vedas* begin with the beginning of the creation and disappear with its disappearance. God begins the creation along with the Vedas. After destruction, they remain in the mind of God who remembers them till the next creation and expresses them on that occasion. Unlike *Mimamsa* and *Nyaya*, *Advaita* philosophy does not admit any need to prove the absoluteness of the *Vedas*. The *Vedas* are self-proved.

The relation of Reasoning and Scriptures

The Relation of *Tarka* and *Srti*, i.e., reasoning and scripture, is an important question in the context of *Advaita* philosophy. Sankaracharya sometimes favours one while at other times he seems to favour the other. On the other hand, sometimes he considers reasoning as much better than scripture. At one place he says that reasoning is based upon the help of scriptures. He gives several arguments against the validity of dialectical reasoning. Of these some important ones are:

1. If reasoning is left to its own course, it may prove anything. Hence it should be based upon scriptures.
2. Due to the difference in the intelligence of persons, a man's reasoning may be refuted by another's more cogent reasoning.
3. Reasoning cannot take us anywhere. We cannot hold an assembly of the logicians of the past, present and future to decide about the truths reasoned out by them in different ways.

Against the above arguments refuting the validity of reasoning, Samkara anticipated the following objections:

1. Reasoning is required even to criticise the validity of reasoning.
2. Reasoning is necessary to decide what is true from among the mutually contradictory statements of the scriptures.
3. If a man's reasoning can be refuted by another's more cogent reasoning, it is because self-criticism is a characteristic of reasoning.
4. Even the scriptures have admitted the validity of reasoning. Yaksha, the author of *Nirukta*, has said that reasoning itself is the seer.
5. If reasoning does not take us to any definite conclusion.

After anticipating these arguments in favour of reasoning, Sankaracharya admits that reasoning has validity at least in some cases though he does not admit that reasoning is valid in the case of Brahman. Thus sometimes Sankaracharya favours scriptures while at other times he supports reasoning.

According to Prof. R. D. Ranade, Prakasanand, and Govindanand, Sankaracharya has given a higher place to scripture than to reasoning. According to Prof A. C. Mukherjee, Sankaracharya has maintained reasoning to be higher than scripture. But he further points out that both reasoning and scriptures are based upon reasoning and reasoning alone decides about their validity.

Metaphysics

The Brahman

Maxmuller has rightly said that the entire Vedanta philosophy may be summarized in a line, "Brahman is true, the world is false and the *jiva* and Brahma are not different... " According to Sankaracharya, Brahman is the highest transcendental truth. It is the ultimate *summum bonum* of human efforts and the basis of knowledge. The ultimate Reality is non-contradictory. It is perfect and the only truth. It is existent, beginningless and unchanging. It is the highest knowledge. By the knowledge of Brahman, the knowledge of the world, which is really ignorance, disappears. Hence, the knowledge of the Brahman is the eternal truth. Brahman is the essence of all things. It is the only ultimate existence. It is unconditional and self-illumined. Hence, it is non-dual, attributeless and unconditioned.

According to Sankaracharya, only the attributeless (*Nirguna*) Brahman is the ultimate truth. The *Upanishads* have described Brahman both as attributed and attributeless. The former has been called the Apara Brahman, while the later has been called Para Brahman. The Para Brahman is unconditional, without particulars and qualities. The Apara Brahman is conditional, with particulars and qualities. Existence, Consciouness and Bliss are the characteristics of Para Brahman. Ramanuja has accepted the ultimate Brahman to be both attributed (Saguna) and attributeless. But according to Sankaracharya, it is ignorance to admit two forms of Brahman since in reality only the attributeless is true. Due to ignorance it appears as attributed Ishwara and limited *jiva.*

According to Sankaracharya, there is no distinction between the self and Brahman. Both are beyond the senses, the mind and the intellect. Whatever is in the self is also in the not-self. By this synthesis of the Brahman and Atman, Sankaracharya negated all types of dualism and established a metaphysical, epistemological and axiological non-dualism. Brahman is present everywhere in the form of the soul. As a matter of fact, according to Sankaracharya, the creation and the destruction of the world have only pragmatic importance. From the transcendental standpoint only the Brahman is the ultimate truth. It is the self. Due to ignorance, it is seen as the individual, the world and the God.

Brahman is beyond the world of name and form. In it there is no appearance and disappearance. In spite of thus admitting Brahman to be beyond all distinctions, Sankaracharya has not taken it to be a negation or *nihil.* Brahman may be realised by immediate intuitive knowledge. Brahman is of the nature of bliss. But this is merely an object of experience. Hence by being called bliss, Brahman does not become attributed. Really speaking, Sankaracharya's distinction of Brahman here is in the sense of "*Neti Neti.*" Brahman is existent because it is not non-existent, conscious because it is not unconscious and blissful because it is not of the nature of pain. It is identical, because it is beyond time. It is unchanging, since it is beyond space. Knowledge is not its attribute, but its nature. It is attributeless, because it is beyond all attributes.

Brahman is indescribable. The Upanishads have described it by calling it "Neti Neti". To call it indescribable means that it cannot be described in the pragmatic language, because it is beyond the senses, mind and intellect. Indescribable does not mean unknowable, since Brahman can be realized; only it is not a subject of intellectual concepts. He is the knower, the lighter of the lights, the conscious light and the soul of all. He is self-illumined. Like the sun, he illumines himself and also illumines everything else. It is only by going beyond the universe that the jiva realizes the real nature of Brahman and that of his own inner self.

Ramanuja vs Samkara

According to Ramanuja, Brahman has personality. He is the ultimate person. But Sankaracharya admits Brahman as beyond all distinctions and impersonal. He is beyond personality. He is neither knower nor doer, but pure knowledge. He is Being not Becoming. He is beyond desires and purposes. Hence, the Brahman of Sankaracharya is beyond the God of Ramanuja.

In Sankaracharya's philosophy, the main proof for the existence of Brahman is the spiritual experience. But as a philosopher, Sankaracharya has tried to advance systematic arguments to prove the existence of Brahman. Of these the main are the following:

Proofs of God's Existence

1. Proof from Scriptures: Sankaracharya has developed his philosophy on the basis of the *Upanishads, Gita* and *Brahman Sutra.* Hence the verses of these scriptures are the greatest proofs for admitting Brahman as the Ultimate Truth. The great sentences like "I am Brahman"

etc., scattered in different *Upanishads* are proofs of the concept of Brahman in Advaita philosophy. The scripture is the proof of the existence of Brahman, and Brahman is the eternal source of the scriptures.

2. Psychological Proof: After giving the etymological proof, Sankaracharya has said that being self of all the existence, Brahman is known to everyone. Sankaracharya emphasizes the above statement further, and points out that every man feels the existence of his own self and no one is ignorant of it. Thus, it is not only a positive evidence but also negates all evidence in opposition.
3. Teleological Proof: The world is so systematic that its origin cannot be admitted as material. Hence, the very system of the universe is a proof of its conscious cause—Brahman.
4. Brahman as the Original Cause: According to the *Upanishads,* the world has no beginning. It is the reflection of the Ultimate Reality. This Ultimate Reality is the original cause of Brahman. Hence the existence of Brahman as the Ultimate cause of the universe is self-proved.
5. The Proof of Immediate Experience: The intellectual proofs regarding the existence of Brahman are only helpful in understanding him intellectually. But beyond the mind, intellect and senses, the only valid proof for the existence of Brahman is immediate experience. By immediate experience all dualism disappears and one realizes the non-dual Brahman, it is the object of spiritual practice. It is not proper to try to understand the entire

Advaita philosophy by means of reason alone. It is only after direct experience that one may grasp the essential meaning of Vedanta. According to the *Upanishads,* Brahman is an object of experience and the intellect should not reason about it. Hence the saying that "Silence is Brahman".

God as Creator

In the philosophy of *Sankaracharya*, the world is merely a reflection of the Ultimate Reality. In fact neither the individual nor the universe nor God have any existence apart from Brahman. From the transcendental standpoint all of them are equally false. Hence, the question of creation is merely a pragmatic problem and God has been brought in only to solve it; otherwise, there is neither a creation nor a creator.

In fact, the *attributeless* Brahman is the only reality. Brahman is pure, transcendental, free, eternal and unconditioned. Brahman covered with Maya, is Iswara or God. God is the reflection of Brahman. Apart from Brahman he is nothing. Brahman is impersonal, while God is the ultimate person. He is the creator, sustainer and destroyer of the physical universe. *Prakrti* is God's power. Creation and destruction are the different stages of the beginningless universe. God requires no instruments to create the world. He creates the world by His power of Maya. He has no purpose in creation, because He is perfect. The world is His *Lila.* The creation is His nature.

Sankaracharya holds that the *jivas* make efforts for liberation. God is eternally liberated and helps the *jivas* in their efforts. The *jivas* are active, but it is God who gives them initiative. The *jivas* are enjoyers, but God is free. Thus, the *jivas* are worldly, while God is beyond the world. But ultimately, all this dualism disappears by the realization of Brahman. According to Ramanuja, however, this dualism is not due to ignorance, it is eternal. Between *jiva* and God there is the relation of part and whole, of the controlled and the controller, of modes and substance.

The Self

Sankaracharya has not admitted any dualism between the self and the Brahman. Self is without particular characteristics. It is itself Brahman. It is all-pervading and omnipresent. It is one, non-dual, partless, beyond space-time, ultimate and true. As a matter of fact, Sankaracharya has described Brahman, self and liberation almost is the same terms.

The Doctrine Of Maya

Avidya or Ignorance

According to Sankaracharya, the scholars have called the behaviour based on *Avidya* as ignorance, while the understanding of the real essence of things is said to be *vidya* or knowledge. Ignorance or *Avidya* is neither existent nor non-existent. It is indescribable. All the objects of the empirical world are due to ignorance. Ignorance is false knowledge. It is the cause of the power of *Maya.* It overshadows the self and the Brahman. It remains in the *jivas* in the form of *karmas.* It is due to ignorance that the *jivas* does not know his real form. Ignorance is eternal and natural, but it can be destroyed through knowledge.

Maya and *Avidya*

***Avidya* and *Maya* are the subjective and objective forms of the same phenomenon. *Avidya* is in the *jiva*. It is the characteristic of its intellect. *Maya* is the creative power of the world of name and form. As knowledge dawns, ignorance disappears but *Maya* is eternal like Brahman, since it is the power of attributed Brahman i.e., *Iswara*. As a matter of fact, just as there is identity between self and the Brahman, similarly *Maya* and *Avidya* are the same.** Both are personal and universal. The words *Maya, Avidya, Adhyasa* and *Vivarta* have been particularly used in almost the same sense. But some of the post-Samkarite Vedantins have distinguished between *Avidya* and *Maya.* According to them, *Avidya* is negative and in the individual, while *Maya* is positive and all-pervading.

From the point of view of education it seems imperative for the teachers and students of education to understand clearly the concept of *Maya* propounded by Sankaracharya. Ignorance and *Maya* are synonyms for Sankaracharya therefore one must know how to dispel ignorance by understanding *Maya* in its right perspective. It will not only help them to attain eternal freedom which is the only goal of all human beings in this world from every kind of philosophical viewpoint but also necessary to lead a happier life which all humans desire in this world.

Maya and *Iswara*

The Brahman together with *Maya* is Iswara. *Maya* is its power. It is the origin of the world of name and form. Names and forms are neither existent nor non-existent. The world is merely a play or *Lila* of Iswara.

Idea of Liberation

Samkara's ideas on liberation have great bearing on education. His commentary on *Brahman Sutra* provides an elaborate description of the nature of liberation. Liberation or *Moksa* is the transcendental truth. The disembodied state is liberation. The liberated self regains his form in the *Advaita Brahma Siddhi. Moksa* is said to be the liberation of the self from ignorance. According to Chitsukharcharya, liberation is the attainment of incessant bliss. It is eternal. The self is eternally liberated. Hence, nothing new is gained in liberation, since otherwise it shall be non-eternal.

As a matter of fact, there is hardly any demarcation line between the achievement of knowledge and liberation. The *Upanishads* have maintained that the knower of Brahman becomes Brahman. ***Moksa*** **means seeing the self in all. It is the status of identity with Brahman. From the transcendental standpoint, the self, the Brahman and the liberation are the same. The self is Brahman. It is eternally liberated. Liberation is the annihilation of the awareness of multiplicity. As the covering of ignorance is removed from the liberated soul, one knows one's real essence. This is liberation.**

Liberation is not due to knowledge but it is knowledge itself. From the point of view of right education Sankaracharya's views on liberation are highly imperative as until one possesses true knowledge one cannot reach liberation. Hence liberation from ignorance is absolutely necessary from every aspect of human life including human freedom which should be the only goal of all education.

Moksa and *Nirvana*

Just as Sankaracharya's Brahman is different from the *Sunya* of the Madhyamika philosophy, similarly *Moksa* is different from Nirvana. *Moksa* is not negative. It is bliss. Like the *Apavarga* of *Nyaya*, in the *Moksa* of Vedanta the self does not become conscious but rather appears as the pure consciousness which is its real nature. According to Ramanuja's qualified monism, in liberation the self does not become *Iswara*, but appears like Him, lives in His contact, dwells in His country and remains attached to Him. But in Advaita Vedanta, the liberated self sees everyone in the self and nothing else. Unlike the Buddhist conception of Nirvana, in the *Moksa* of Advaita the self is not annihilated but only its conditions are destroyed, the liberated self is non-different from Brahman. *Moksa* is not attained through self-purification, since self-purification is an activity. *Moksa* is attained through knowledge. It is not an activity, but existence itself. *Moksa* is eternal, pure in nature like that of Brahman.

Liberation While Living

Sankaracharya believed in the possibility of *gradual liberation (Krama Mukti)*. Commenting on a verse in *Prasnopanishad* regarding the concentration on Om, he says that such concentration leads to Brahman Loka where we gradually attain complete knowledge. At another place, Sankaracharya has maintained that worship of the attributed Iswara leads to purification from sins, the attainment of bliss and gradual liberation.

According to Sankaracharya, Moksa does not mean the cessation of body, but the extinction of ignorance. Hence, he believes in liberation even while living (*Jivan Mukti*). Just as the

wheel of a potter remains moving even after the pot is made, similarly the man goes on living even after attaining liberation, because there is nothing to stop the earlier continuity of life. Sankaracharya has here given the example of a man who sees a double moon due to some defect in the eye and cannot stop seeing like this in spite of knowing that in fact there is only one moon. Thus, from the point of view of education Samkara's concept about liberation is of great importance.

Ethics in *Advaita Vedanta*

According to some critics, "the *Advaitavada* of Sankaracharya has no place for ethics as it raises the supreme ideal of life above good and evil". Thus, it has been pointed out that there is no place for ethic's in Sankaracharya's philosophy. **According to Sankaracharya, Brahman is the self, while the world is unreal. The ultimate end of man, according to Vedanta, is the attainment of Brahman consciousness. Thus, Brahman is beyond the dualism of right and wrong. It is beyond all dualism, Man's aim, according to Advaita Vedanta, is to reach a status of non-dualism, because dualism is Maya or *Avidya* while non-dualism is the Brahman or Reality. Kant has also pointed out that dualism of right and wrong should be seen on the moral plane.**

On the moral level, man must have both the alternatives of right and wrong, but he must voluntarily choose the right only. Under no circumstances he should choose the wrong. Ultimately he needs to choose the right due to his innate nature. If there is any conflict between the two in his mind, he is not on the moral level. Thus, as a moral philosopher points out, "Virtue lies in its antagonist". This analysis amply clarifies that the summum bonum of man in Samkara's philosophy is beyond ethics. This is

also highly relevant to the field of education as all education aims to help humans to choose the right only by dispelling the wrong.

Samkara was not a great philosopher but an equally great social reformer. He roamed about the country from North to South, and East to West, preaching the philosophy of Vedanta and making every effort to reform the society. It is only on the transcendental level that Samkara has negated all dualism. On the pragmatic level, the dualism of the right and wrong is as true, as all other dualisms. Before in the achievement of liberation, man must have due consideration for right and wrong, but after liberation is achieved, such a consideration becomes superfluous, because the liberated person, essentially established in the Brahman consciousness, does only that which is always right as it directly flows from the ultimate good, the Brahman. Such a concept of Samkara is highly relevant to our education in all times.

Questions

1. In what way does Advaita Vedanta's epistemology help humans to attain the right path in life? How is it connected with education?
2. Though Ramanujam and Samkara aim at liberation but their approaches are different just as their concepts regarding Brahman are different. In what way are their approaches towards attaining liberation helpful in the pursuit of right education? Comment briefly.
3. Samkara's concept of Maya is synonym to that of ignorance. How can right education help students to get a closer view of Maya or ignorance to make them lead a contended and happier life in this world which is also one of the goals of education?

4. Enumerate Samkara's ethical views and explain how such views are related to good education.
5. In what manner Samkara's and Ramanujam's philosophical persuits are helpful in improving our educational systems in the modern times? Comment briefly.

PART - II

Overview

Most of the thinkers, philosophers, educationists and revolutionaries given under here have been great educationists too as they expressed about education certain ideas they strongly felt good. These great philosophers, idealists and unparalleled literary contributors reflected directly or indirectly on the educational themes with the view that if their ideas were taken into consideration they could bring tremendous changes and help improving the realm of education. In that way their contributions possess immense value. I have tried to present their educational ideas along with some details of their lives without which the reader would have not learnt what made them think for education that way. Some of these ideas have also been highlighted for the benefit of the reader.

Chapter I

Sri Aurobindo Gosh

Aurobindo Gosh was born on the 15th August in 1872 at Calcutta now known as Kolkata. His father Dr. Krishandhan Gosh was a famous physician and was totally immersed in the western way of life. As such he provided all his three sons a western kind of education dominated with western ways and culture implicit abundantly with good knowledge of English language. Aurobindo was a dedicated student since his early age. He was sent to a convent school at Darjeeling for his primary education. At the age of seven in 1879 he was sent to England to pursue further studies. Later on he studied at St. Paul's School in London from 1884 onwards. He graduated from High School in 1890 and obtained good marks at the examination. Immediately after that he got admission at the King's College for further studies. Subsequently he also passed the ICS (Indian Civil Services) examination but was declared not successful on account of not taking part in the horse-riding examination. Since he got excellent marks in the theory examination at the ICS, he was given another chance to take part at the horse-riding examination. But he declined to take it as he did not want to be a subservient to the British who were the masters of the country at that time. Aurobindo deliberately refused to take the riding test for he had immense love for his country.

Master of Many Languages

His brilliance and dedication during his studies at the college endeared him to many of his teachers in England. Gradually he developed as a great linguist and besides English he also learnt French, Spanish, Italian, Greek and Latin languages. When he came back to India he mastered Sanskrit and excelled in Bengali, Marathi and Gujarati languages too. At the national level there seems to be no other person who has been such a great linguist like him.

A Nationalist and Revolutionary

He was a great revolutionary thinker and a nationalist from the very outset. When he was very young he anyhow conceived the idea that revolutionary changes were going to take place in the world in a very near future. He also thought that he was sent by Him to play some important role in that. But he remained outside the country for a long time waiting for the right chance to come to participate in the country's independent movement. As a preparatory movement he took part in the anti-British movement by delivering several revolutionary lectures at 'Bhartiya Majlis'. It was the time when some devoted Indians including him, took a secret oath that they would always abide by their country and work for its independence. After a short time from that event, he came down to India and constantly worked against the British rule. His anti-British activities did not go unnoticed for long by and consequently he was arrested on the May 2, 1908 and was sent to the Alipur Jail.

During his incarceration at the Alipur Jail, Aurobindo devoted most of his time to studying the *Gita*, *Upanishads* and practising yoga. When he was released from the jail, he found that most of the nationalist leaders were in jail and the entire country was drowned in an environment of great disappointment. In view of that he continued his anti-British activities with further vigour and delivered regular lectures at different important places in the country before huge multitudes. The British were constantly keeping an eye upon him but before he was rearrested he left finally for Puducherry where he lived for forty years until he died. Thus, Puducherry became his second home where he gradually grew as a spiritual leader of the country.

A Spiritual Leader

During his long stay at Pudicherry, he kept close contacts with the revolutionaries of the country but now his way of participating in the revolutionary movement was altogether different. He was now taking part in the movement like a visionary and a spiritual leader. Consequently his influence on the youth of that time and even subsequently has been very wide and deep. He deeply desired that an individual needed to be changed first from within before he took part in other activity. On the first Independence Day **on 15th August in 1947 at the ashram, he reflected upon his 'five visions' which he thought highly imperative for the people of India. These were: (i) United and Free India (ii) Freedom to all the Asian people and their positive role in advancing human culture (iii) An United Nations that could be helpful in building human dignity and prosperity (iv) India's role as a spiritual leader of the world (v) Development of mankind to a stage from where they would grow as enlightened human beings and lead a spiritual life, subsequently shunning all social evils and discriminations. Such a vision of Sri Aurobindo is the testimony of his high and spiritual way of thinking and his love for his countrymen as well**

as for the world community all over the world. He started having such spiritual visions just before he started practising yoga in jail.

A Distinguished Teacher

In view of his revolutionary activities which were laced with spirituality, he can very well also be known as a world leader who was primarily a great thinker, an enlightened teacher and a nationalist as well. **Besides being a great philosopher, he was a great teacher too. He taught at different places in some leading colleges in India. He believed that a good teacher must possess great human and spiritual qualities with which he could constantly go on changing and influencing his students. A good teacher must know his students thoroughly and consequently he should try to bring changes into them. He held that a teacher normally had three ways to redeem his students: These are: (i) an influencing manner of teaching; (ii) constantly providing examples before the students to bring positive changes in them, (iii) exerting his/ her personal influence on the pupils.**

Perhaps such thoughts of Sri Aurobindo in the field of education are highly pragmatic for they provide a great promise to help pupils to be good human beings before they are anything else. No education at any level can afford do without following his extraordinary reflections which not only provide a procedure but also promise good results which are utterly needed by education at all levels in our country today.

Questions

1. In view of Sri Aurobindo's abandoning participating in revolutionary activities physically and moving to Puducherry for good to accelerate the freedom movement, do you take him as a realist or pragmatist? Comment critically.
2. What were Sri Aurobindo's five visions? How do these visions influence the realm of education?
3. How does Sri Aurobindo express his views to help teachers redeem their students? To what extent do you agree with him? Comment critically.

Chapter 2

Mohandas Karamchand Gandhi

Early Life

Mohandas Karamchand Gandhi was born on October 2, 1869 at Porbandar, a small city state on the coast of the then Gujarat region of Bombay Presidency. His father, Karamchand Gandhi held the position of *diwan* or prime minister in the court of the prince of Porbandar. Mohandas loved and respected his father but was closer to his mother, Putlibai, who was saintly and practised self-denial. She often gave herself willingly to the service of others and the needy. Mohandas got his early education at Rajkot, where Karamchand had moved the family. He was extremely shy during his early school days. He would rush to and from school without talking to any of his classmates. At the age of 13 he married a pretty but strong-willed girl, named Kasturba, who was almost of his age.

Unfortunately Karamchand Gandhi died when Mohandas was only 17 years old. Mohandas was in college at that time. His family hoped that he would follow in the career of his father. When Mohandas became unsuccessful in the first term at the college, a friend suggested an alternative to him. He said: why not go to England for further study? **His mother was however worried that he would be corrupted by certain loose European practices. But she permitted Mohandas reluctantly only after he had sworn**

three vows—that he would abstain from meat, abjure alcohol and avoid women. Therefore, almost at the age of 19 he sailed for England in September 1888 leaving Kasturba and his first son, Harilal, behind.

Man in the Making

After some early difficulties to stay as a vegetarian, Mohandas joined a group of people known as the London Vegetarian Society. **The Society members first introduced him to the *Bhagavad Gita*, an epic poem and a sacred prayer-book. Mohandas admitted with embarrassment that he had never read it before. He also read the Old Testament but was not inspired by it. However, when he read the Sermon on the Mount and Jesus' doctrine of turning the other cheek, the idea of non-violence struck him deeply.** Gradually he learnt the ways and means of living in England with peace and consequently worked very hard to get a degree in law from England.

While he was coming back home he learnt that his beloved mother died. On his return to India, he realized that although he had studied law in England, he had not learnt how to practise it. He did not have the knowledge of Indian law that a lawyer in India needed. In view of that and without good prospects of a job in his own country, Mohandas Gandhi took an offer from a local Moslem mercantile firm with branch headquarters in the British colony of South Africa. **It was at this time that once while Gandhi was travelling by train through South Africa to Pretoria, a white man entered the first-class compartment in which Gandhi was also sitting. The white man summoned two officials who pushed Gandhi along with his luggage out of the first-class compartment. It ignited a spark of revolution in Gandhi's mind to fight against the British atrocities**

and discrimination, first in the South Africa and later on in India.

Further Transformation

In 1894 Gandhi founded the Natal Indian Congress based on the model of the National Congress in India. It provided him an opportunity to organize the Indian community in South Africa. He once urged the Indians to first make their self-improvement by attaining three things in certain areas. These were: sanitation, education and cooperation. When he returned to India in 1896, he held regular public meetings reflecting the dismal conditions prevalent in South Africa. Gandhi's such selfless efforts created a lot of influence on the Indian common man who was also desirous to get redeemed from the British rule. During these few years Gandhi travelled to India and South Africa many times. **Each time when he travelled to India or to South Africa the thought of self-restraint gradually became stronger within him. Meanwhile John Ruskin, a British essayist of the 19th century, influenced him a great deal. The principles that Gandhi derived from Ruskin were: 1. The good of an individual is contained in the good of all. 2. A lawyer's work has the same value as the barber's, in as much as all have the same right of earning their livelihoods from their work. 3. A life of labour—the life of the tiller of the soil and the handicraftsman—is the life worth living.**

Such unique ideas, which Gandhi had never thought before, brought in him a new transformation and influenced his life style permanently. He was now increasingly intent on devoting himself to the service of others. A true life of serving others, he now started believing, required to give up all possessions. He thought that even his body should exist to serve others and not be tempted with personal comforts. Consequently he restricted

his diet to uncooked foods. He also started to engage in fasts. But it was not too easy to leave possessions and to train the mind to give up things willingly. At first it was a slow and painful process. Then he turned to the *Bhagavad Gita* that he had first discovered in London. It became his guide to lead a spiritual life for the remaining part of his life.

Gandhi felt he could no longer fully keep up his responsibility to his family if he would give over completely to the public service. Ties to children and wife interfered with a life required for that. **He thought, 'true service would require both celibacy and poverty'. Consequently at the age of 37 in 1906, Gandhi took a vow to abstain from sexual relations. He kept the vow for the rest of his life.** After constantly struggling against the British atrocities in the South Africa for some years, he finally came back to India in January 1915. G.K. Gokhale, an eder statesman and nationalist leader, was his guide initially. Though Gokhale died only seven months after he met Gandhi, he left an indelible mark on Gandhi's mind. He said, 'Spend your first year with your ears open and your mouth shut.' It was a great advice, which Gandhi followed strictly. Gandhi travelled across India in filthy, jam-packed third-class compartments wearing a dhoti. Peasants came from far and wide to have his *darshan* (have a look on him). Then he settled down in an ashram on the banks of the Sabarmati on the outskirts of Ahmedabad. Traditionally a retreat for the religious, Gandhi's ashram was a self-supporting community like the earlier Phoenix and Tolstoy Farms. The residents had to swear to be true to Gandhi's principles. They had to abstain from eating meat, sex and alcohol. They were also required to take a pledge against 'untouchability'. Ashram residents addressed Gandhi as *Bapu*, which meant father. Rabindranath Tagore, the Noble Prize-winning Indian poet described him as "The Great Soul in Peasant's Garb". Soon people started calling him 'Mahatma.'

Dawn of a New Idea

While staying at the *ashram* Gandhi had several opportunities to fight for the poor and the peasants whenever their rights were threatened by their masters. Once while he was in Ahmedabad, he was called in to arbitrate a wage dispute between mill owners and workers. Both sides respected him. In fact some of the mill owners were sponsors of Gandhi's ashram. The strike of the workers continued for two weeks when the morale of the strikers almost broke down. Without money to buy any food for the family, the workers wanted to return to work. It was easy for Gandhi to tell them to hold out, but he was not in their position to understand their plight. At this time Gandhi was struck with a new idea. He announced to the workers that he would fast in their support. This was his first public fast to support the cause of the needy and the down trodden. Later on he continued fasting in moments of political crisis throughout his life. The British rulers yielded to Gandhi's cause—not necessarily because they shared Gandhi's point of view but because they didn't want to be responsible for his death. The new idea worked very well for the cause of the Indians and the country's freedom.

Non-Cooperation & Non-violence

After constant struggle against the British to get freedom for the country Gandhi never felt defeated. If one idea did not work at times, he thought of another one to fight them. Now it was 1920 when Gandhi thought of a new idea and desired to put into action. It was non-cooperation, which meant a boycott of everything British—law courts, jobs, schools and clothing. He also saw it as an influential way to attract the world attention to the cause of Indian freedom. He also told his people that non-cooperation along with non-violence would bring home rule within a year if Indians followed it earnestly. At first the British government thought very little of non-cooperation but as time passed Gandhi's both ideas shook the British government terribly. At times riots erupted and a great number of Indians were killed but non-violence as a tool proved very effective. In spite of mass arrests and even after Gandhi was also imprisoned without charges or trial, non-violence prevailed. Non-violence with a determined and persistent effort was used as Satyagraha (civil disobedience), which involved hundreds of Indians marching against the British laws.

Gandhi's Influence and Education

The rest of the story is known to the world. Gandhi's persistent efforts did not only bring freedom to the Indians but his impact was felt all over the globe. It is a fact that the struggles of other Asian and African countries to gain independence from the colonial powers were greatly influenced by his work. Gandhi's life and work has captured the imagination of new generation. Gandhi cannot be ever forgotten. **In this age when many nations possess the capacity to destroy life on earth, Gandhi's example of trust, tolerance and protest by non-violence could prove crucial for all the mankind. Not only in the field of human values to help improve conduct, Gandhi had specific ideas to educate the illiterate masses of India. He insisted that basic education must be given at the beginning of schooling to all without any discrimination. He also insisted that some kind of handicraft must be taught at the school level to make the student self-sufficient and enable him/her to earn the**

daily bread which is a great requirement of this country in view its vast population. Dr. Kothari was greatly influenced by his ideals and consequently he recommended compulsory and free education up to high school to all in the Education Commission he prepared for the country soon after independence.

Gandhi's influence is colossal as far the development of human character is concerned. His ideas regarding celibacy, truthfulness, love for the downtrodden, obedience to the teachers, love for the country and selfless help to the poor and needy are matchless. One can trace ***Bhagwad Gita's*** influence on him in his efforts to bring Hindu-Muslim unity, practising non-violence, service to the poor and needy without possessing any idea of returns to such services. In his ashram at Sabarmati he washed his own clothes, cleaned toilets and inspired people to help themselves and detest the idea of untouchability. What we need in India today is to make our youth learn how to help themselves, learn the dignity of labour and foster love for the people of other religions. India is a nation where people of different sects and religions live. This country cannot develop strong physically, emotionally and spiritually unless people possess friendly feelings for each other. In this respect Gandhi's ideas would always prove highly beneficial if followed earnestly.

Questions

1. What incident in South Africa changed Gandhi's way of thinking? What were its positive effects for South Africa and consequently for India?
2. To what extent did Ruskin's ideas influence Gandhi and helped him develop his ideology to get freedom in India? Discuss briefly.

3. What was the impact of the *Bhagavad Gita* on Gandhi? How was such an impact instrumental in providing him the strength of character he needed to help his people to get freedom from British rule?
4. Why did G.K. Gokhale tell Gandhi 'to hear only and speak nothing for one year' before he would indulge in the struggle for freedom? Comment briefly.
5. In what ways have Gandhi's principles influenced the realm of education? Do people really follow his ideas after six decades of independence?

Chapter III

Jiddu Krishnamurti's Philosophy and his Impact on Education

Family Background and Childhood

Jiddu Krishnamurti was born on May 12, 1895 in a small town of Madanapalle in Andhra Pradesh in a Telugu-speaking family. His father, Narainiah, was employed as an official of the then colonial British Administration. Jiddu was very fond of his mother, Sanjeevamma. Unfortunately, she died when he was only ten. After retirement, Narainiah sought employment at the Theosophical Society office that had headquarters at Adyar. Eventually he moved his family to Adyar in January, 1909.

Just after a few months when the family had moved to Adyar, that Krishnamurti first met C.W. Leadbeater who claimed clairvoyance. At the nearby Adyar river beach, Leadbeater had noticed that Krishnamurtui had the most wonderful aura he had ever seen before. This strong impression was different to Krishnamurti's outward appearance, which, according to eyewitnesses, was pretty common and unimpressive. The boy was also considered dim-witted and often possessed a vacant expression. Leadbeater remained unshaken and he strongly believed that the boy would become a spiritual leader, a great guru as well as an orator. Following Leadbeater's 'discovery', Krishnamurti was taken under the leadership of the Theosophical

Society. Leadbeater and a small number of trusted associates undertook the task of educating and preparing Krishnamurti as the '*vehicle*' of the expected 'World Teacher'. Both, Krishnamurti and his younger brother Nitya were privately tutored at the Theosophical Society in Madras and later they were carried abroad to continue their education further. In spite of his number of problems with school work and concerns about his capacities and physical condition, the fourteen-year-old Krishnamurti, within six months, was able to speak and write in English.

During this time, Krishnamurti had developed a strong bond with Annie Besant and viewed her as a replacement to his mother. After a prolonged legal battle with Narainiah, Besant took custody of the boy and his brother Nitya. Gradually, due to his separation from the family and home, Krishnamurti and Nitya became extremely close. In the following years they often travelled together. In the meantime Theosophical Leadership in 1911 established a new organization called the ***Order of the Star in the East*** to prepare the world for the already mentioned '*Coming*'. Krishnamurti was named as its head. Membership was open to anybody who accepted the doctrine of the *Coming of the World Teacher.*

The Spiritual Awakening

Krishnamurti and Nitya were taken to England for the first time in April 1911, when he gave his first public speech, to young members of the Order. Between that time and the start of World War I in 1914, they also visited several other European countries, where Krishnamurti delivered a number of lectures. In the beginning he was described as a hesitant and repetitive speaker, but there was steady improvement in his delivery and confidence, and he gradually took command of the meetings. While travelling from Sydney to California they lodged at a cottage relatively secluded at Ojai Valley in California. Both found the Ojai Valley to be very agreeable, and eventually a trust formed by supporters purchased the cottage and surrounding property for them. It henceforth became Krishnamurti's official place of residence. In August during1922 at Ojai, Krishnamurti went through an intense, 'life-changing' experience. It has been invariably, characterized as a spiritual awakening, a psychological transformation, and a physical conditioning. Those around him would refer to it as *'the process'*, which continued, at very frequent intervals and varying forms of intensity, which Krishnamurti narrated that (awakening) until his death in the following way.

'...I was supremely happy, for I had seen. Nothing could ever be the same. I have drunk at the clear and pure waters and my thirst was appeased. ...I have seen the Light. I have touched compassion which heals all sorrow and suffering; it is not for myself, but for the world. ...Love in all its glory has intoxicated my heart; my heart can never be closed. I have drunk at the fountain of Joy and eternal Beauty. I am God-intoxicated.'

Similar incidents continued with short intermissions until October. Later such incidents eventually resumed regularly, always involving varying degrees of physical pain to mark the start of the *'process'* accompanied by what is variably described as *presence*, *benediction*, *immensity*, and *sacredness*. It was reportedly often felt also by others who were present there.

In the next few years Krishnamurti's new vision and consciousness continued to develop. New concepts appeared in his talks, discussions and letters, along with an evolving vocabulary that was progressively free of Theosophical terminology. The main themes in his meetings started to be different from the well-defined precepts of Theosophy. It would be *Happiness* one year, *Questioning Authority* the next, or *Liberation* the following. His new direction reached a climax in 1929, when he refused to continue with the *Order of the Star*. Krishnamurti dissolved the Order at the annual Star Camp on August 3, 1929 at Ommen, in Netherlands, where, in front of Annie Besant and several thousand members, he delivered an extraordinary speech. He told people that they didn't need to follow any guru, if they wanted to grow. In fact, he believed that man has to transcend to reach the truth. Truth does not come down itself to meet man.

Leadbeater and other Theosophists expected the *vehicle* to have certain telepathic experiences but mystified by these developments they were at a loss to explain the whole thing. During his later years, the continuing *process* often came up as a subject in private discussions between him and his closest associates. These discussions shed some light on the subject, but were ultimately inconclusive regarding its nature and origin. According to a biographer the process at Ojai was an overwhelming mile stone in Krishnamurti's spiritual progress. Something new had now occurred for which his training had not entirely prepared him. A burden was lifted from his conscience. He took his first step to become an individual. In terms of his future role as a teacher, the process was his bedrock. It had come to him alone and provided him with the soil in which his newfound spirit of confidence and independence could take root.

Break with the Past

Krishnamurti denounced all organized belief, the notion of guru and the whole teacher-follower relationship. Instead he inspired man to work totally as a free person. Whenever he was asked to clarify his position, he gave answers asserting that all such questions were irrelevant and stated them vague. He eventually disassociated himself from the Theosophical Society, its teachings and practices, despite being on cordial relationship with many of its members throughout his life. He would often refer to the totality of his work as '*the*' teaching and not *my* teachings. His concern was always about *the* teachings and not anything else. He reflected once purposely:

'All authority of any kind, especially in the field of thought and understanding, is the most destructive, evil thing. Leaders destroy the followers and followers destroy the leaders. You have to be your own teacher and your own disciple. You have to question everything that man has accepted as valuable, as necessary.'

Impact on Education

Krishnamurti's impact on educations has been colossal. He died on Feb. 17, 1986 at the age of 90. During this period of time the first of several schools based on Krishnamurti's educational ideas opened in India. **Proper holistic and the overall rearing of children into *sane, whole* individuals, free of conflict had been one of his major and continuing concerns**. These schools and others in India and elsewhere continue operating under the patronage of Krishnamurti Foundations even today.

Krishnamurti introduced many new concepts and terms which became recurrent themes in later talks and discussions. Such themes are highly imperative to the field of education and are related to man's mental growth. One such idea is the *choiceless awareness*, a type of awareness that is from *moment to moment*, without the implicit or explicit choices that accompany judgments. Another new concept was his challenge of the existence of *a division between the conscious and the subconscious mind, maintaining that such division is a man-made one, and that in reality there is only a single consciousness.* Perhaps spurred by the relative isolation at Ojai, and the long sessions of meditation he was engaging daily, he started talking about *right meditation.* He would touch on this subject in practically every subsequent talk or discussion. Most of his above referred views are obviously highly related to 'the awakening of human intelligence'. He distinctly reflected on it in the following manner:

To awaken that intelligence there must be the deep urge to know but not to speculate. Please bear in mind that what to me is a certainty, a fact, must be to you a theory, and the mere repetition of my words does not constitute your knowledge and actuality; it can be but a hypothesis, nothing more. Only through experimentation and action can you discern for yourself its reality. Then it is of no person, neither yours nor mine.

Gradually his lectures became highly thought provoking and metaphysical. **His subject matter evolved to encompass several new and different concepts: the idea that individuality is an illusion, the notion that true love, beauty, peace, and goodness, had no opposites** – such duality being only a construct of thought and the need for a *radical mutation.* As his lectures gradually became metaphysical oriented, it led to the changing of audience and its outlook. In the early 1970s he mentioned that his approach represented an unfolding of something new. But the fundamental teachings remained unchanged. In late 1980, he took the opportunity to reaffirm the basic elements of his message in a written statement that came to be known as the ***Core of the Teaching***. An excerpt follows:

The core of Krishnamurti's teaching is contained in the statement he made in 1929 when he said: 'Truth is a pathless land'. Man cannot come to it through any organization, through any creed, through any dogma, priest or ritual, nor through any philosophical knowledge or psychological technique. He has to find it through the mirror of relationship, through the understanding of the contents of his own mind, through observation, and not through intellectual analysis or introspective dissection. Man has built in himself images as a sense of security—religious, political, personal. These manifest as symbols, ideas, beliefs. The burden of these dominates man's thinking, relationships and his daily life. These are the causes of our problems for they divide man from man in every relationship

Thus, for almost 90 years until his death he continued his intellectual discourses to enlighten people, who came to attend his lectures and who desired to know answers to difficult questions. He is said to be the Buddha's incarnate and like him he also discoursed with the audience. He dispelled all the vague questions and refused to answer them just like the Buddha, telling people that those questions were just meaningless and would not bring any concrete knowledge to them. **In order to keep human mind alert and free from biasness, he said that one has to be free from three things. These are: identification, comparison and condemnation—i.e. no strong leaning, attachment or detachment towards anybody, not to compare things unnecessarily, and not to criticize or condemn things or people for no reason. It would help not only to keep one's mind away from negative thinking but will help keep it free providing it freedom to think correctly. Perhaps it is one of his greatest gifts to the realm of education and to the teachers today, as most of our education has been suffering from an environment**

created by inadequate and immature thinking of the teachers and the educators.

Questions

1. Why did Krishnamurti dissolve the Order of the East? What arguments he presented before the people while dissolving the Order? Does his talk that followed the dissolving the Order has any bearing on education?
2. What new ideas Krishnamurti presented before the people after the 'awakening'? How they influence education?
3. What reflections Krishnamurti made for perfecting human intelligence? Do you agree with him? Comment objectively.
4. What three things he wants humans to be free from? How are they useful to the students ands teachers? Give your dispassionate opinion.

What is Krishnamurti's actual message to the teachers? Does his message affect our current educational practices? Discuss briefly.

Chapter IV

Rabindranath Tagore

Early Life

The youngest of thirteen surviving children, Rabindranath Tagore was born in Kolkata of parents Debendranath Tagore and Sarada Devi on 7th May in 1861. He was largely raised by servants, as his mother had died in his early childhood. He often declined classroom schooling, preferring to roam the mansion or nearby places Bolpur, Panihati, and others. Upon his *upanayan* (initiation) at age eleven, he left Kolkata on 14 February 1873 to tour India with his father for several months. They visited his father's Santiniketan estate and stopped in Amritsar before reaching the Himalayan hill station of Dalhousie. There, he though young, read biographies and was home-educated in history, astronomy, modern science, and Sanskrit. He also examined the poetry of Kālidāsa at that time.

A prospective barrister, Rabindranath enrolled at a public school in Brighton, East Sussex, England, in 1878. He read law at University College London, but left school to explore Shakespeare and more. He returned to Bengal in 1880 without obtaining any degree from London. On 9 December 1883 he married Mrinalini Devi who gave birth to five children, two of whom died before reaching adult age. In 1890, he began managing his family's vast estates in Shilaidaha, a region now in Bangladesh, where he was joined by his wife and children later on.

Knighted by the British

Tagore left Shilaidaha in 1901 and moved with his family to Santiniketan to found an ashram which grew to include a marble-floored prayer hall (The Mandir), an experimental school, groves of trees, gardens, and a library. His wife and two of his children died there after some time. His father too died on 19 January 1905. By now, his readership among Bengali and foreigners grew tremendously. It was in Santiniketan that Tagore published such works as *Naivedya* (1901) and *Kheya* (1906). He also translated some of his poems into free verse. He learned on 14th November 1913 that he had won the 1913 Nobel Prize in Literature, and had become the first Asian Nobel laureate. The Swedish Academy appreciated the idealistic nature of a small body of his translated material that included *Gitanjali: Song Offerings*, which he wrote in 1912. Tagore was also knighted by the British Crown in the year 1915. **In 1921, Tagore and an agriculture economist Leonard set up the Institute for Rural Reconstruction, later renamed Santiniketan—'Abode of Peace'—in Surul, a village near the ashram at Santiniketan. He sought aid from donors, officials, and scholars worldwide to 'free villages from the shackles of helplessness and ignorance'. He criticized India's 'abnormal caste consciousness' and untouchability and lecturing against these, he penned untouchable heroes for his poems and dramas. He campaigned successfully to open Guruvayoor Temple to Dalits (untouchables), who were not permitted by the rigid caste system to enter the temple so far. He largely mourned the poverty of Calcutta and condemned the growing socioeconomic decline of Bengal.**

Tagore's last four years were marked by chronic pain and two long periods of illness. He often lost consciousness during that illness. During late 1937 he once remained comatose and near death for an extended period. This was followed with a similar spell three years later in late 1940. He never recovered from that. After an extended suffering, he died on 7 August 1941 in an upstairs room of the Jorasanko mansion in which he was raised.

Touring the World

Between 1878 and 1932, Tagore visited more than thirty countries on five continents, many of these trips were crucial in familiarizing non-Indian audiences to his works. In 1912, he took a bundle of his translated works to England, where his writings impressed missionaries, Charles F. Andrews, Anglo-Irish poet Yeats and others. Indeed, Yeats wrote the preface to the English translation of *Gitanjali*, while Andrews joined Tagore at Santiniketan. He then began touring the United States and the United Kingdom during 1912. From May 1916 until April 1917, he went on lecturing in Japan and the United States and denounced nationalism. His essay '*Nationalism in India*' was largely scorned and yet praised by the pacifists, including Romain Rolland.

Though known mostly for his poetry, Tagore also wrote novels, essays, short stories, travelogues, dramas, and thousands of songs. Of Tagore's prose, his short stories are perhaps most highly regarded. His works are frequently noted for their rhythmic, optimistic, and lyrical nature. His stories are mostly borrowed from deceptively simple subject matter: common people. Tagore wrote eight novels and four novellas, among them *Chaturanga*, *Shesher Kobita*, *Char Odhay*, and *Noukadubi* are worth noticing. They deal with rising

Indian nationalism, terrorism, and religious zeal clad in the Swadeshi movement which Tagore's hardly appreciated. His *Gora* raised controversial questions regarding the Indian identity.

Tagore's Versatility

At sixty, Tagore took up drawing and painting. Successful exhibitions of his works—which made a debut appearance in Paris after being encouraged by certain artists he met in the south of France—were held throughout Europe. His works sought to articulate, in Tagore's words, 'the play of feeling and not of action'. In 1890 he wrote *Visarjan* (Sacrifice), regarded as his finest drama. The Bengali-language originals included intricate subplots and extended monologues. Later, his dramas probed more philosophical and allegorical in themes. These included Dak Ghar. Another is Tagore's *Chandalika* (Untouchable Girl), which was modelled on an ancient Buddhist legend describing how Ananda—the Gautama Buddha's disciple—asked water of an Adivasi (untouchable) girl.

The *Sadhana* period, 1891–1895, was among Tagore's most yielding time. **He associated his earliest stories, such as those of the *Sadhana* period, with an exuberance of vitality and spontaneity, the traits cultivated by the zamindar Tagore's life. Seeing the common and the poor, he examined their lives with a depth and feeling singular in Indian literature up to that point.** In *The Fruit-seller from Kabul*, Tagore speaks in first person as a town-dweller and novelist who chances upon the Afghani seller. **Tagore's poetry varies in style and form. It contains classical formalism and is highly visionary. He is totally awed by the mysticism of the *rishi*-authors who—including Vyasa, the Bhakti-Sufi mystic Kabir, and Ramprasad Sen. Yet his poetry became most innovative and**

matured after his exposure to rural Bengal folk music. These—rediscovered and popularized by him, resemble 19th-century *Kartābhajā* hymns that emphasize inward divinity and rebellion against religious and social orthodoxy.

Tagore responded to the mostly crude emergence of modernism and realism in Bengali literature by writing experimental works in the 1930s. Examples of such works include *Africa* and *Camalia*, which are among the better known of his latter poems. He occasionally wrote poems using *Shadhu Bhasha* (a Sanskritised dialect of Bengali). Later on, he began using *Cholti Bhasha* (a more popular dialect). Other notable works include *Manasi*, *Sonar Tori* (*Golden Boat*) and *Balaka* (*Wild Geese*). *Gitanjali* is Tagore's best-known collection, winning him international fame and the Nobel Prize.

His Reflections on Education

He criticized the Swadeshi movement, denouncing it in *The Cult of the Charka*. He emphasized self-help and intellectual uplift of the masses. He reflected frankly that the British imperialism was a political symptom of India's social disease, and **urged Indians to accept that 'there can be no question of blind revolution, but of steady and purposeful education.' Tagore condemned rote schooling. He said it was like a 'parrot's training', in which birds were caged and forced to feed upon pages torn from books until they died. These views led him while visiting Santa Barbara in October 1917, to conceive of a new type of university, desiring to 'make Santiniketan the connecting thread between India and the world'. He thought of 'a world centre for the study of humanity somewhere beyond the limits of nation and geography.**

He is thus, the first Indian who reflected that all educational efforts must end up aiming at internationalism. The school, which he named Visva-Bharati had its foundation stone laid on 22 December 1918. It was later inaugurated on 22 December 1921. Here, Tagore implemented a *brahmacharya* pedagogical structure employing gurus to provide individualized guidance for pupils. Tagore worked hard to raise funds for and staff the school, even contributing all of his Nobel Prize money. Tagore's duties as steward and mentor at Santiniketan kept him busy. He taught classes in mornings and wrote the students' textbooks in afternoons and evenings. He also fund-raised extensively for the school in Europe and the U.S. between 1919 and 1921.

Tagore's relevance can be gauged by festivals honouring him: *Kabipranam*, Tagore's birth anniversary, the annual 'Tagore Festival' is held in Urbana, Illinois, in the United States. *Rabindra Path Parikrama* walking pilgrimages takes place from Calcutta to Shantiniketan and ceremonial recitals of Tagore's poetry is held on important anniversaries. Nobel laureate Amartya Sen saw Tagore as a 'towering figure', being a deeply relevant and many-sided contemporary thinker. His Bengali-language writings published in the 1939 known as *Rabīndra Rachanāvalī*, is also considered as one of Bengal's greatest cultural treasures. He has rightly been proclaimed as the greatest poet India has produced.

Tagore's wide appeal [may stem from the fact that] he speaks of longings for perfection that we all possess in some way. It indicates his idealistic nature which is branded with his deep-rooted naturalism. He awakens a dormant sense of childish wonder, and saturates the air with all kinds of enchanting promises for the reader. Santiniketan is a symbol of his deep attachment with nature and his artistic mannerism which he wanted to cultivate

among his students not only in Santiniketan but throughout the country and later on internationally. We can thus summarize his educational approach as naturalistic, realistic as well as leading to spiritualism, which is largely reflected in his *Gitanjali*, the best of his creations. As a great human being he possessed extreme love for his fellow beings and composed poetry for all those who were downtrodden and Dalits. His efforts endure in his vast canon and in the institution he founded, Visva-Bharati University. 2011 will be the 150 birth centenary of Tagore and to make it a real success both Indian and Bangladeshi governments have decided to work jointly. Part of the birth centenary celebration would be the Indian goverment's bid to get Santiniketan the university town, an UNESCO heritage site tag. Thus, Tagore's dream of developing internationalism through education is not far from fulfilment.

Questions

1. What themes are predominant in Tagore's early poems? Is there any connection between this thinking and with the establishment of Santiniketan ashram he founded later on to offer education to all? Comment briefly.
2. Tagore believed in internationalism instead of nationalism—that he condemned several times reflecting about it in his poems. What steps did he take to propagate his ideology? How far does he seem to have succeeded in his efforts to extend internationalism through education?
3. Examine Tagore's main educational ideas and their relevance to education in modern times.
4. Tagore is primarily a naturalist but at times his views also match idealism. Where do you place him out of the two isms? Explain with suitable examples.

Chapter V

Swami Vivekananda

Early Life

Vivekananda was born in Shimla Pally, Calcutta on January 12, 1863. He was given the name Narendranath Dutta by his father Vishwanath Dutta, an attorney at Calcutta High Court. Vishwanath was a generous, liberal and progressive person and possessed a broad outlook in social and religious matters. Narendranath's mother, Bhuvaneshwari Devi possessed a pious disposition, practised austerities and prayed to Lord Shiva to give her a son. She reportedly had a dream in which Shiva promised her to give her a son.

Narendranath's personality was greatly influenced by his parents—the father, by his rational mind and the mother, by her religious temperament. He learnt the power of self-control from his mother and often quoted in his later years: 'Remain pure all your life; guard your own honour and never tarnish the honour of others. Be very tranquil, but when necessary, harden your heart.' He was reportedly adept in meditation and could enter instantly the state of Samadhi. In the state of Samadhi he would often see a light and a vision of Buddha.

Narendranath had varied interests and a wide range of scholarship in philosophy, history, the social sciences, arts, literature, and other subjects. He showed much interest in scriptural texts, *Vedas*, the *Upanishads*, *Bhagwad Gita*, *Ramayana*, *Mahabharat* and the *Puranas*. He was also well versed in classical music, both vocal and instrumental. Since boyhood, he took an active interest in physical exercise, sports, and other organizational activities. Even when he was young, he questioned the validity of superstitious customs and condemned discrimination based on caste system. He also refused to accept anything which did not have any rational proof.

Meeting Sri Ramkrishna

Fortunately he came to Ramakrishna in search of a guru and soon became his disciple. Ramakrishna taught him Vedanta Philosophy stressing that all religions were true and service to man was the most effective worship of God. After Sri Ramakrishna died Vivekananda became a wandering monk, touring India to get a first-hand account of the country's dismal condition. He also toured different parts of the world and lectured there on Hinduism and its different aspects. He also sailed to Chicago in 1893 and represented India as a delegate in the Parliament of World Religions.

Parliament of Religions

The Parliament of Religions opened on September 11, 1893 at the Art Institute of Chicago. On this day Vivekananda gave his first brief address. He represented India and Hinduism. Though initially nervous, he bowed to Saraswati the goddess of learning and began his historic speech with, 'Sisters and brothers of America!'To these words he got a standing ovation from a crowd of seven thousand. The ovation lasted for two minutes. When silence ensued he began his address and greeted the youngest of the nations in the name of 'the most ancient order of monks in the world, the Vedic order of sanyasins, a religion which has 'taught the world both tolerance and universal acceptance.' He quoted two illustrative passages in this relation, from the *Bhagavada Gita*: 'As the different streams having their sources in different places all mingle their water in the sea, so, O Lord, the different paths which men take, through different tendencies, various though they appear, crooked or straight, all lead to Thee!' Despite being a short speech, it voiced the spirit of the Parliament and its sense of universality.

Dr. Barrows, the president of the Parliament said, 'India, the mother of religions was represented by Swami Vivekananda, who exercised the most wonderful influence over his auditors.' The *New York Critique* wrote, 'He is an orator by divine right, and his strong, intelligent face in its picturesque setting of yellow and orange was hardly less interesting than those earnest words, and the rich, rhythmical utterance he gave them.' The *New York Herald* wrote, 'Vivekananda is undoubtedly the greatest figure in the Parliament of Religions. The American newspapers reported him as "the greatest figure in the parliament of religions" and "the most popular and influential man in the parliament".

He spoke several more times at the Parliament on topics related to Hinduism and Buddhism. All his speeches had one common theme—Universality and stressed religious tolerance.

His extraordinary address to the American audience won him a great honour. As an eloquent speaker he was invited to several forums in the United States and spoke at universities and clubs. He conducted several public and private lectures, installing Vedanta, yoga and Hinduism in America, England and a few other European countries. He also established Vedanta societies in America and England and later sailed back to India where he founded the Ramakrishna Math and Ramakrishna Mission, a philanthropic and spiritual organization in 1897.

Vivekananda's Influence

In a short span of 39 years he awakened and inspired many to follow his precepts. His most famous statement was 'Arise, Awake and Rest not till the goal is achieved.' Today many people of different nationalities, religions, races, colours, sects and creeds follow the teachings of Vedanta he introduced in late 19th and early 20th centuries. He is most popular among adults. Present day youth and many aspiring souls seek inspiration from his teachings and messages even to date. While living Vivekananda, proclaimed that though he would leave his body like discarding his clothes, he would continue to work towards the upliftment of all humanity. After departing from this world he is believed to have interacted with great souls to fulfil his work. He gave a new direction to religion by transcending ritual concepts of religions and promoted formless and nameless meditative practices like Raja Yoga and Spirituality. Swami Vivekananda is regarded as one of India's foremost nation-builders. His teachings influenced the thinking of other national and international leaders.

Vivekananda is most popular among young adults. Present day youth and many aspiring souls seek inspiration from his teachings and messages even to date.

Ideas Related to Education

1. It had always been in Narendra's nature to test something thoroughly before he would accept it. Thus, he held that

developing the faculty of reasoning among the youth is one of the pioneer tasks of education so that no pupil accepts anything without testing it.

2. Initially, Narendranath revolted against idol worship and polytheism and did not agree with Sri Ramkrishna's worshiping the Kali, the Mother Goddess. Narendranath tested Sri Ramakrishna several times but the guru never asked him to abandon reason. He faced all of his arguments and examinations with patience. Then he said to him patiently, 'Try to see the truth from all angles'. It could be the role of a teacher even today to ask him/her to see things dispassionately if the disciple does not agree with him on certain accounts. Just rejecting pupils' questioning would neither enlighten them nor provide them any understanding. This aspect is perhaps highly being neglected in the process of our education at all levels in our country these days.

3. During the course of five years of Narendra's training under Sri Ramakrishna, Narendra was transformed from a restless, puzzled, impatient youth to a mature man who was ready to renounce everything for the sake of God-realization. The duty of a guru is always to transform his disciples to lead him to maturity just as Sri Ramkrishna did with Narendranath. In time, Narendra accepted Sri Ramakrishna as guru, and when he accepted, his acceptance was whole-hearted, with complete surrendering to the guru. The teacher's role is to transform the disciple and when once the transformation is done, the disciple must accept his guru and his teachings wholeheartedly.

4. Vivekananda taught that service to men was the most effective worship of God. There cannot be a better goal of education than serving human beings, barring no caste or religion. It is also one of the most important precepts of the *Bhagwad Gita* which Swami Vivekananda constantly hammered on the minds of Indians.
5. As a religious wanderer and pledged to help the needy of every caste mainly, the down trodden, Vivekananda never lagged behind in fulfilling his mission in life. Like a missionary he was always ready to support the weak and the needy. He constantly propagated such ideas for the benefit of teachers and the good of pupils. Could there be any better mission of education today than what Vivekananda taught us 'to help the needy of every caste and religion, specially the down trodden?
6. Once he remarked, "Education must exploit the hidden talents in the pupils". It would not only help him/her getting enlightened but will also aim at developing certain skills and talents. In that respect he was not only an idealist but a pragmatist as well.
7. He would accept an idea only when it appeals him completely and only when he is certain that it would bring some kinds of benefit to him. Therefore, from the beginning he relied upon reason. Sri Ramkrishna did not interfere with Narendra's sticking with 'reason' but he also told him to try to see the truth from all angles. It was an approach to widen the narrow horizons of one's mind.

8. Abovc all Swami Vivekananda helped restore a sense of pride amongst Indians, presenting ancient Indian teachings in their purest form to a Western audience, which so far knew nothing about the spirit of tolerance implicit in the religion. It is one of the foremost tasks of a teacher, in the view of Vivekananda, to cultivate tolerance and a sense of self-pride among students. Perhaps it is one of the most important tasks of education to free every Indian from a feeling of subservient and to build in him/her a sense of self-pride by cultivating in him/her sense of dignity.
9. His most famous statement was 'Arise, Awake and Rest not till the goal is achieved.' It is highly a positive statement that could develop a strength of will among our teachers as well as in our students and also help them to attain their goals in life.
10. Swami Vivekananda's ideas have had a great influence on the Indian youth. In many institutes, students have come together and formed organizations meant for promoting discussion of spiritual ideas and the practice of such high principles. Many of such organizations have adopted the name Vivekananda Study Circle. One such group also exists at IIT Madras. Additionally, Swami Vivekananda's ideas and teachings have carried on globally, being practised in institutions all over the world.

Questions

1. What was the most positive influence of Sri Ramkrishna on Swami Vivekananda? How did he gradually initiate Vivekananda in his own ideology and train him as he

desired? Provide examples to justify your views? Do you agree that a teacher in India should seek parallel ideology and help his/her students to grow in life in that manner?

2. What gave Swami Vivekananda a standing two minutes ovation at the Parliament of Religions held at Chicago? What were his best ideas projected before the Parliament of Religions and which of those ideas you deem fit to be upheld in the classroom when you work as a teacher?
3. Quote some of Swami Vivekananda's best educational ideas that you consider utmost and very important to be accepted at all levels in Indian Education. Discuss briefly.

SECTION B

Western Philosophical Systems

Chapter One

Philosophy and Education

What is Philosophy?

The meaning of the term philosophy can be derived from Plato's Republic. He says, "He who has a taste for every sort of knowledge and who is curious to learn and is never satisfied may be just termed a philosopher." He states further, "A philosopher is a lover, not of part of wisdom only, but of the whole." Nothing can be left out by a philosopher. He considers all sorts of knowledge to be his province. He desires to see life steadily and seeks it whole. When once Glaucon asked Socrates, "Who are the true philosophers?" he replied, "Those who are the lovers of the vision of truth." The knowledge which a philosopher loves to possess shows him the eternal nature of the truth, which does not vary from generation to generation and is not corrupted by time.

This leads us to consider that it is the reality itself, which is the subject of philosophical inquiry. Philosophy in the past has always enquired into the questions about the nature of life, nature of man, his origin, destiny and the goal of his strivings. The philosopher seeks knowledge in order to find answers to all these questions. It may be said that all who have attempted sincerely to provide answers to fundamental matters, possess some degree of consistency and rationality, have a claim to philosophical rank, whether they are biologists, theologians or agnostics. Thus, the early thinkers who defined natural phenomenon, the nineteenth-century scientists who sought their explanation in terms of atoms, motion and energy, religious people of all ages who have discovered the direct intervention of God in human affairs, all have been philosophers as they have tried to provide a reasoned-out point of view on these fundamental matters.

Philosophy, therefore, is an inquiry into fundamental matters. It is a search for knowledge. The philosopher not only tries to answer the difficult and vital problems of life, but also attempts to synthesize all knowledge in order to find the whole truth. Brubacher states, "Indeed one would fail to be true to the spirit of philosophy, if he did not try to reduce his manifold convictions to some single, inclusive, consistent scheme of thought."

Thus, the more a philosopher tries to know the more, nearer he comes to some basic principles of experience, which he applies and practises in his own life. Therefore, philosophy results in action. Dewey remarks, "Whenever philosophy has been taken seriously, it has always been assumed that it signifies achieving a wisdom which would influence the conduct of life. Witness the fact that almost all ancient schools of philosophy were also organized ways of living…" Philosophy has a direct and most intimate relationship with the quick look on life. It leads men to adopt a way of life, which would lead them to a distinct and well-sought goal. In this way, philosophy results in the adoption of a certain definite desired way of life. If a man has a philosophy of life, it becomes of some use to him. A certain belief about life is not merely an academic matter, but an example, which could enlighten and redeem men from getting lost in a quandary.

What is Education?

Education can be defined as an art of 'leading out', which would mean that the whole of education—intellectual, moral, emotional, physical, consists of leading out the innate knowledge, including the virtues and powers of the child. The Latin dictionary defines the word 'educere' meaning 'to lead out' and 'educare' meaning 'to bring up' and 'to raise'. It is from the latter word that the term education has been derived. Education thus, consists of the modification of natural development of an individual, without which he would have been different. That means that when education process begins, it brings some sort of influence on the pupil. The modern concept 'that the best education consists of withholding all influences from him is entirely a different approach. It contains the idea of freedom for the young ones. Interference by adults is completely rejected, because it would bring distortion into the child's personality.

Education has also been defined as the dynamic side of philosophy. This is, whatever we contemplate for the wholesome development of the child we put that into practice, meaning educating him correctly. John Stuart Mill defines the notion of education to the culture which each generation purposely gives to those who are to be its successors, in order to qualify them for at least keeping up, and if possible for raising, the level of improvement which has been maintained. According to Mill, education is a purposeful process or influence, which implies a personal educator. James S. Ross views educational process consisting of two persons—the educator and the pupil. He thinks that like a magnet education has two poles; it is a bi-polar activity. At the one pole there is the educator and at the other end there is the pupil or the 'educand'. Adams has suggested the word 'educand' meaning the person to be educated. John Adams sums up his views on education in the following manner.

Education is a bi-polar process in which one personality acts upon another in order to modify the development of the other. The process is not only conscious but also a deliberate one. The educator has the clearly realized intentions of modifying the development of the educand. The means by which the development of the educand is to be modified are two:

(i) the direct application of the educator's personality to the personality of the educand and,

(ii) the use of knowledge in its various forms.

One of the important aspects of education is its aims. In fact, the aims are the crystallized notions or aspirations of a society which formulates them to provide direction to the growth and development of its people. It is the modification of the direction of the already framed goals. However, the direction of the child's growth has never been the same since the ancient times. Different centuries have formulated and witnessed different educational ideals or aims in the light of their own needs. Thus, the aims of education are determined by the needs of a society and when once the aims are finally formulated, they provide direction to the growth of the child. Aristotle said: "Educational aims are correlated to the ideals of life", and therefore, as these ideals diverge due to the passage of time and needs of people, the educational aims also diverge. During the early medieval period, Loyola, the founder of the Society of Jesus, expressed ardently that one should always strive to reach 'the glory of God.' Milton, during the seventeenth century reflected that the end of learning is 'to repair the ruins of our first parents by regaining to know God aright and out of that knowledge to love Him, to imitate Him, to be like Him…'

During the nineteenth century, Herbert Spencer asserted that the aim of education 'is complete living.' In this way, different centuries have witnessed different proposals of aims formulated by various educators. But the great educationists have been great philosophers too, and thus, there has been a great relationship between philosophy and education. In fact, education is conceived as the other side of the same coin of which one side is philosophy. Let us now examine the relationship between philosophy and education in an elaborate way.

Philosophy and Education

The relationship between philosophy and education has been from the earliest times. The philosophers, from ancient to modern times, have tried to focus their attention on all aspects of education. In a sense, this is only to be expected, for it is impossible to investigate the phenomenon of existence or ask questions about the best way for mankind to live, without giving some consideration to topics concerned with the intellectual, aesthetic and moral development of individuals. Once we embark on a consideration of such matters, we are squarely in the domain of educational philosophy and theory as well.

After answering questions relating to the nature of 'goodness and how men can achieve a good life', Plato sets to explain how all that could be incorporated into an educational system, which would help bringing up the good and just society. Plato's *Republic* is recognized as one of the greatest educational treatises, which contains a system of educating people, who could be converted into philosophers if they adhere to the schemes of education suggested by him. There are other examples in the history of education wherein we find great philosophers reflecting upon the pedagogical aspects in order to bring change to the traditional and obsolete educational systems.

Kant, St. Augustine, and John Locke, recognizing the importance of educational theory have reflected upon it in their writings to provide better ideas for the improvement of educational themes and problems. John Dewey, the leading philosopher of the twentieth century, thought that the study of education was one of the most important tasks that could be undertaken, and even a life time could be devoted to it. Thus, philosophy and education are closely linked, and the relationship between them, have been expressed by philosophers of all times. It would not be out of place to mention that most of the educational theory has evolved out of philosophical reflections. In recent years, however, philosophy of education has been recognized as a distinct branch of philosophy. Since then it has undergone modification. Let us now examine what philosophy of education is.

Philosophy of Education

Our sense of purpose or lack of it, will lead us to act in a particular direction. Our concepts of values and our vision of the totality of existence will mould us and affect our relationship with other people. If we believe that there are spiritual values and there is an earlier life and the present life is a preparation for it, our aim and practice of education are likely to be affected by such ideas. Traditional psychology has reflected much on the issue mentioned above. But the approach to the realm of philosophy of education in modern times is less metaphysical and more practical. Philosophy now is viewed more as a technique of criticism, thinking and clarification. Not everyone is prepared to reduce it to a department of logic, but few are anxious, on the other hand, to make it a synthetic, or synoptic, overall system of life's purpose, and then apply it to education. Now philosophy is used in a somewhat empirical and practical way for discussing and probing current educational problems.

Looking at its empirical and practical ways, the modern approach to educational philosophy is quite different from what it has been in the past. Today, words and phrases like 'equality', 'quality of opportunity', 'total education', 'integration' and 'discipline', and problems of moral education and curriculum are all the subject matter of philosophy of education. The distinctive feature of philosophy of education is to remain concerned with forms of thought and arguments expressed almost in a Socratic manner like, 'What do you mean?' and 'How do you know?' including to find out the fundamental basis of 'our forms of awareness' and the grounds of human knowledge.

Scope of Philosophy of Education

The scope of philosophy of education may be stated with reference to three central and important areas of concern, each of which has a distinctive contribution to make to the study of education.

(i) Elements of Philosophy

The current components of philosophy have special contribution to make to the philosophy of education and the study of education in general. Whether in the area of metaphysics, epistemology, logic, or ethics, classical and modern philosophers have tried to answer questions which are of direct relevance to education.

(ii) Philosophical Analysis

The use of analytical technique has been in vogue in recent times. This approach to philosophy of education has gained importance in most recent times and is now widely applicable in the educational arena. It consists of the application of the techniques of linguistic analysis to the examination of educational concepts and ideas.

(iii) History of Educational Theory

In dealing with such topics as human knowledge and learning, the philosopher will need to enrich his study with examining what philosophers of different times have had to say on these topics. The ideas of the great thinkers such as Plato, Aristotle, Kant, Aquinas, Dewey can throw light on many contemporary issues in education. An approach through the 'schools of philosophy'—examining the views of the Idealists, the Naturalists, the Realists and so on—can make a rich contribution to the philosophical treatment of educational problems.

Questions

1. What is Philosophy?
2. Trace the impact of Philosophy on Education.
3. What are John Adams views on Education?
4. What is the scope of Philosophy of Education?

Chapter Two

Elements of Philosophy

Metaphysics

Prior to the twentieth century, philosophers did not often possess much to state and analyze what they thought they were doing. It was taken for granted that philosophy was important and they knew well what its job was. Traditionally, philosophers thought they were doing something like:

(a) giving an account of the world in the most general possible terms;

(b) giving an account of reality (that is the real world, as opposed to the world of appearance);

(c) giving an account of the world and man's place in it.

To provide such an account of the world and reality is to engage in metaphysics. The word metaphysics comes from the Greek expression *tametaphysica* meaning 'things beyond the physical realism'. The early Greek philosophers, Plato and Aristotle, attempted to devise a hypothesis which accounted for all scientific knowledge as well as something else which would help us to know about the universe. The early philosophers were broadly divided into two groups as far as defining the universe was concerned. There were those who thought that the universe was in a permanent, static state, and those who thought that it was in an ever-changing state or flux. Heraclitus, for instance, believed that change was inevitable, while Parmenides opposed him and stated that reality was an unchanging phenomenon. Democritus, who can be reckoned as holding a middle path, tried to reconcile the conflict between these two types of groups and developed his theory of materialism. Its chief proposition was that the ultimate constituent of the real world was an indivisible physical unit, the atom, which remained permanently the same. However, atoms were constantly moving in space, colliding and sometimes combining the form of matter. With such explanations Democritus attempted to accept both the 'permanence' and the 'change' theories about the structure of the universe.

But during the centuries that followed Aristotle, the scope of metaphysics was considerably enlarged. Therefore, in the light of its extended scope, let us try to know its other interesting features which are the outcome of the later centuries. Such features are cosmology, the nature of man, the soul, the extent of man's freedom of action, notions about a supreme being, teleology, the nature of reality and ontology.

Cosmology

Cosmologists have tried to study the origin of cosmos from the point of view of a cause and effect relationship. In this extent the oldest views are those of the theologians, who believe that God is the first cause of the physical world. Their contention is that there lies an unending orderliness and design in the extended universe. Such orderliness and perfection cannot be achieved by anyone else except God.

Counter views have been expressed by the evolutionists, who express the view that the universe contains an infinite variety of forms. Charles Darwin, in his theory of evolution expresses the view that the universe has developed as a result of gradual evolution, which has taken place out of the principles of selection and struggle for existence.

(i) Body-Mind-Relationship

In the western world, the idea of the dual nature of soul and body has been reckoned throughout the past centuries. The spiritualists believe that mind is more fundamental and that the functions of body depend on it. But philosophers like Descartes contend that mind and body are 'really distinct'.

During the nineteenth and the twentieth centuries philosophers' views on the soul (mind) body relationship changed. They now believe that although body and mind are two different kinds of reality, both can affect each other.

(ii) Nature of Man

The study of man has been of great importance since the time of Socrates. Man is the only known agent who has been inquiring about the universe and his own place in it. The idealists take man as a spiritual being. The naturalists believe that man is merely a biological phenomenon. They do not make any distinction between the self and the body. The experimentalists like Dewey define self in relation to his social environment. They think that man interacts with his social world and is capable of changing events and discovering his own value system.

(iii) Freedom of Man

The oldest view in this respect is known as determinism, which says that man is not a free being. He simply acts as commanded by forces greater than himself. In Hinduism there is a belief in reincarnation and predestination. Christian philosophers like St. Augustine and Calvin believed in the doctrine of predestination.

Determinism is condemned by the theory of freewill. The *Gita* upholds the view of free-will. Those who believe in freewill, propound that man has the power of choice and the capability to take the initiative and can design his own destiny. Such thinkers assert that freewill exists and man can choose better things to mould his future. But according to John Dewey thinking is akin to the 'operation of knowing', which is a 'natural response of organisms'. It can be selected, analyzed or synthesized.

(iv) God's Existence

Metaphysics has also tried to deal with the question of God's existence. Those who have faith in God are known as theists and their philosophical reflection about Him are acknowledged as theism. The theists believe that the cosmos exists through Him. 'In a restricted sense, the term theism also stands for monotheism. The Christian and Muslim philosophies are based on the existence of one Supreme Being. St. Augustine's efforts to establish intellectually the probability of God have been sustained and reinforced, by St. Thomas Aquinas. The Quran says that there is no God but Allah. *"La ilaha-il-Allah"*

Some of the ancient beliefs conceive reality or God's having polytheistic nature. Such a view is known as polytheism. Tribal people believe in spirits and gods and the stories of Roman and Greek gods and goddesses have not been entirely forgotten.

There is another conception of God, which is known as deism. In it, God is reckoned to have created the universe and human beings as well, but having done so He exists apart from all of them. Philosophers like Aristotle have such a belief in Him and His creation. There is yet another conception about Him. It is that God is everything and everything is in Him. It is called pantheism. The Vedas contain such a belief. Besides, in the western world pre-Socratic schools of thought also believed in pantheism.

Exactly opposite to the belief about His existence, there is the belief in God's non-existence. Such believers or atheists do not conceive any thought about the existence of any kind of Supernatural Being. The Carvaka's philosophy is the most ancient Indian materialistic school of thought in which ideas of heaven or hell and belief in God are totally rejected. Existentialists like Jean Paul Sartre have expressed thoughts in which God is dethroned from His original position. The philosophy of Marxism is based on such anti-godism.

Teleology

The metaphysical study which reflects on the question, whether or not there is any purpose in this universe, is broadly called 'teleology'. Such a view is directly opposite to the views which contend that the world is an outcome of sheer accident and that there exists a sort of blind mechanism which explains the movements and development of world. Teleology refers to the view that there has been a purpose in the universe right from the beginning.

Ontology

Ontology or the philosophy of being can broadly be divided into three categories: naturalism, idealism and pragmatism.

In naturalism the existence is explained as matter or physical energy, which occupies space and time. While in idealism the spirit, which is identified to God, is reckoned as the only reality. The pragmatists' belief is that everything is in a state of flux in this world, which is 'characterized throughout by process and change'.

So far the traditional metaphysics give a metaphysical account of the world. But all that role of metaphysics is found to be rejected in the modern times. Consequently a new role for philosophy has been found out. The most important factor has been the rise of modern science and the realization that its success has been due to the *refusal to accept any views (about the world) which are not supported by evidence*. 'Giving an account of the world in the most general terms' has come to seem a better description of science than of philosophy.'

The logical positivists have accused the metaphysicians of discovering the answers to the difficult issues such as, 'whether life exists in other galaxies or not?' They argue that such issues can only be solved by the empirical methods of science. Therefore, the metaphysics have been accused that its process has been idle and simply speculative.

Besides, metaphysical reflections pose to say something true or false about the world, when in fact the outcome is nothing. That means that such reflections literally lack sense. Metaphysical statements can be refuted by a principle of verification, according to which something can be accepted as true, if it can be verified. Therefore, philosophy or metaphysics can provide us with no knowledge about the world. It has no subject matter. Instead, it is just a method of logical analysis of language. Philosophy is, therefore, an activity through which the meaning of statements is revealed, and by means of science they are verified.

In spite of the fact that the approach to the study of metaphysics has not been considered the same in modern times as it was in the past, it has several implications for education. A historical survey of metaphysics provides abundant enlightenment about the important human problems, which have been an enigma to men. Besides, although in recent years philosophy has been reckoned as an activity to reveal the meaning of statements, its importance has never diminished as its role is to provide logical analysis and define the obscure concepts and difficult statements.

Epistemology

Epistemology is that branch of philosophy which concerns itself with the theory of knowledge and deals with the questions about how knowledge is acquired. The extent of knowledge and how one can be certain of what one claims to know is the field of epistemology.

How Knowledge is Acquired

The problem of knowledge has been debated by philosophers since ancient times and many times several possibilities of acquiring it have been known. Philosophers, in general, have considered four positions on the possibilities of acquiring knowledge.

One of the views of acquiring knowledge is that of sceptic thinkers, who have a questioning attitude towards the possibility of having knowledge. The philosophy of scepticism originated from the ancient Greece. The early Greek thinkers like Protagoras stated, "no more such than such". He further stated that none of us knew anything, not even that "whether we know or we do not know". Such trends in thinking laid the foundation of skepticism. At a much later date David Hume reflected that knowledge was derived from empirical data by inferences, but, as it cannot be demonstrated, it is uncertain.

Another possibility of knowledge is through agnostic reflection. Agnostics take an extreme negative view and state that any sort of conclusive knowledge of ultimate reality is agnosticism. David Hume, Comte and Santayana are the philosophers who follow the agnostic track in finding knowledge. Most of the agnostics claim that all our knowledge is only symbolic, relative and conditioned.

T.H. Huxley, who first coined the term 'agnosticism' meaning 'not being able to know' applied agnostic principles even to questions like 'whether our knowledge about God is true'. He said that since there is no experimental evidence with respect to the nature of God and His immortality, we must exclude the supernatural from our knowledge.

Yet there are philosophers, who may be called experimentalists, who believe that knowledge is always fractional and can never be achieved in total. It always functions in a present situation or field and we can appropriate such functional and fractional knowledge.

Another area of study in the possibility of acquiring knowledge has been known as 'affirmation of knowledge'. The philosophers who believe in acquiring knowledge through affirmation reflect that 'knowledge of the ultimate' reality is possible. The idealists believe in that way. Plato asserted it by acquiring knowledge through the allegory of the cave in the *The Republic*. Spinoza stated it in the doctrine of substance; Descartes by his idea of *'cogito ergo sum'*.

(i) The Extent and Kinds of Knowledge

Philosophers have broadly categorized the kinds of knowledge in three ways: One kind of knowledge which is based upon observation has been known as a posterior. Pragmatists like John Locke through his principle of *tabula rasa* explain that point. He states that all thoughts which back the reason and provide knowledge are supplied by 'experience' and gradually the 'blank sheet' is filled with impressions.

The domain of knowledge has also been extended through experimental procedures. Though the knowledge acquired through experiments is not regarded as something final or total, but it is something which is reckoned as functional which carries the experience forward satisfactorily. John Dewey considered the procedure of achieving such knowledge by trying and understanding. That is to try an idea in practice and to know the truth of it from the consequences of the result.

There is another theory with respect to the extent and kind of knowledge. It is called 'a priori'. According to his theory knowledge, is treated as self-evident. Kant in his book *A Critique of Pure Reason* has acclaimed 'priori' as the theory of knowledge. He explains that 'general truths must be independent of experience—clear and certain in themselves'. Therefore, principles, when understood, are reckoned to be true. They do not require any proofs either through observation or experiments. One example of this sort of knowledge is mathematical knowledge, which cannot be violated by future or in future.

(ii) Sources and Instruments of Knowledge

There are five instruments of knowledge.

They are: sense-perceptions, reason, intuition, revelation and authority. Sense-perceptual experiences are considered to be the primary instruments of knowledge. Philosophers who conclude that way are called 'empiricists' and the approach is known as 'empiricism'. Thomas Hobbes, Francis Bacon, John Locke, George Barkley and David Hume fall into the line of empiricists.

Another approach to trace the sources of knowledge is that of rationalists whose approach is called 'rationalism'. The rationalists hold that reason is the chief source of knowledge. Socrates was one of the earliest philosophers who advocated the use of reason and the orderly way in thinking. Aristotle, Descartes, Spinoza, Kant, Leibniz—all have been important exponents of rationalisms.

Though 'intuitionism' as an instrument of knowledge is less popular, it is quite an important source of finding knowledge. It is considered to be a great source to discover the truth. Henri Bergson's name is more attached to this approach of finding out the truth. It is believed by the intuitionists that intuition is successful to a greater extent in providing a successful guide line to life enabling it to take wise decisions.

Another instrument of receiving knowledge is revelation. It refers to the process through which God Himself reveals the truth known to man. Examples of revelation are in abundances in the Christian, Muslim and Hindu religions. However, modern scientific views have made people question the beliefs about the idea of revelation.

Yet another instrument of gathering knowledge is through an indisputable authority, such as the holy texts—the Bible, the Quran and the Vedas. It makes authoritarianism closely related to revelation in the sense that the revealed knowledge is certified by an indisputable authority, which is the holy text.

On the educational plain, the conception of knowledge carries a number of important implications. The main task of the educator is the development of knowledge and understanding in the various domains. Therefore, it is very essential that the teacher employs methods which foster the development of the right kind of knowledge in pupils. 'Pupils may have weak knowledge' in that they are in possession of certain facts, say, geography or science, without being able to produce the evidence on which these facts are based. Arguably, much of 'school' knowledge is of this kind; pupils believe things merely because teacher says so. Therefore, the teacher has to be very careful in organizing and providing the knowledge.

Logic

This element of philosophy deals with the fundamental laws of thinking and reasoning. All sorts of knowledge employ thinking to determine whether thinking is accurate or not. Much in this respect will depend upon keeping in line with the laws of logic. The laws of logic determine that the reasons being produced as evidence to reach conclusions are valid or not. Therefore, logic can be defined as the science of good reasoning.

Logic has two main branches, which are concerned with the rules for correct reasoning in various intellectual and educational spheres. One of the branches is known as inductive logic, which concerns itself with making observations of particular instances and inferring conclusions from them. Newton, for example, concluded his principle of 'gravitational force' from the instance of the apple falling from the tree in his garden. In the highly developed physical sciences, inductive evidence may achieve a high level of accuracy and help in establishing theories and laws. In the field of education, inductive reasoning has been of great importance as it is being employed by educational researchers in making particular observations while attempting to reach general conclusions. However, it must not be forgotten that when we use inductive reasoning, we deal with probabilities rather than certainties. That is one of its limitations.

The other branch of logic is deductive logic, which helps making valid inferences from conclusions. It was Aristotle, who first devised the use of deductive logic. The basic form of deductive argument devised by Aristotle is the syllogism which consists of three propositions. The first two propositions are known as premises, which provide reasons for the claim that conclusion is true. The final proposition provides the conclusive results. Its example is given here:

All men are mortal. Idris is a man.) – Premises

So Idris is mortal. – Conclusion

If the inference drawn from the premises is valid, that is if the premises imply the conclusion, we can say that the conclusion as well as the premises are true. But, if any of the premises is false, even though the inference from it seems to be true, the conclusion, therefore, would be false. For example:

All philosophers are men.

David is a man.

So he is a philosopher.

The above inference is invalid because the conclusion does not follow from the stated premises. All who have been philosophers may have been men, but it is not necessary that David, who is a man, is also a philosopher. Therefore all arguments of deductive type must be subjected to careful analysis.

The use of logic is of great importance in the field of education. We must apply logical analysis and the rules of valid inferences to all educational claims so as to be sure of their status. Without applying logic and finding out valid inferences from statements, it is quite likely that one may be caught, into a fallacy or a circular argument. In education, for instance, there are a number of controversial issues on which views are polarized between supporters of comprehensive schools and those who favour selective schooling. Therefore, one has to be careful in drawing inferences from arguments of such a nature.

Ethics

Ethics is the study of human conduct. Philosophers have always been concerned with 'how mankind ought to behave?' and 'what is the best way for man to live?' The field of ethics, therefore, is of great significance for educational philosophers.

There are two main areas concerning ethics with which the philosopher of education may be more concerned. The first is that of moral education, which must hold a central position in any programme of general education. The task of the philosopher is to de-limit the scope of morality and indicate some of the ways which would help thinking to construct coherent ethical theories. Without a clear view of what morality is, educators cannot plan to organize moral educational programme. In this way, it can be observed that moral philosophers may have a practical contribution to the development of moral educational programmes.

The other area of ethics important in relation of education is concerned with the justification of education. In establishing educational activities, all kinds of value judgments have to be made. For instance, what powers and rights are to be given to teachers in relation to their treatment of the pupils; what educational aims ought to be prescribed and what criteria is to be kept in view while framing the curriculum. All decisions in the above referred areas are value judgments for they are concerned with the selection of what is most valuable in the educational system for a generation.

Aesthetics

This philosophical element leads to the study of art and experience of beauty. The term has been derived from Greek. It denotes the study of sense experience generally. Both Aristotle and Plato were interested in the question 'whether it could embody and communicate knowledge and truth'. Truly speaking, Plato was a little apprehensive as to whether the study of aesthetics could communicate knowledge. Much later on, in the eighteenth century, Kant in his *Critique of Judgment*, argued for the importance of aesthetic judgment for it provides enlightenment to connect the theoretical and practical aspects of human nature.

The study of aesthetics can be divided into two main parts. The first deals with the analysis of the theories. For example, the idealist theories that are propounded by Croce and Collingwood come under this category. Second deals with aesthetics and is concerned with the analysis of concepts in art, the concepts of the work of art itself, and the concepts of meaning, intention, representation as well as illusion within arts.

In the field of education, the development of an aesthetic nature among pupils has long been considered as an important part of their education. P.H. Hirst includes the study of aesthetics or 'literature and the fine arts' in his list of seven forms of knowledge, which frame the basis for liberal education. There are other modern educators who consider the study of aesthetics essential and significant for pupils.

Philosophers of education think that there are many useful areas of enquiry in the field of aesthetics, which may assist an educator. For instance, the concept of creativity has gathered importance in recent years. Another area of interest to the educational philosophers in this field is related to 'the development of emotions'. It is reckoned to be an essential aspect of all-round development of a pupil's personality. Philosophers argue that the reading great works of literature can create sensitivity in pupils. Therefore the knowledge of aesthetics is of great importance in the field of education.

Questions

1. Define the elements of philosophy briefly.
2. What does epistemology concern about? What is its relationship with education? What role has the teacher to play to enrich students' knowledge? And how?
3. How is logic helpful in education?
4. Discuss how ethics is related to education.
5. Discuss briefly the nature of aesthetics and how it is useful in the realm of education.

Chapter Three

The Problem of 'What is Good?'

What is Good?

A definition of what is good is difficult to provide. To many people it means something different. What is good could best be said to be relative and subject to change. Plato believed that something was good so long as it agreed with goodness in the world of ideas. Many would not agree with him. Likewise Socrates thought that education and knowledge necessarily produced virtues which in turn produced happiness. To him knowledge was the key to all things and it led to goodness and happiness.

An opposite view of life was held by the Hedonists and Epicureans whose motto was "eat, drink and be merry, for tomorrow we would die." They believed in enjoying themselves to the full every moment because they said that pleasure was good and pain was evil. In nineteenth century, a similar philosophy known as utilitarianism was developed in Britain. Its basic definition of virtue was "the greatest happiness of the greatest number". One of the leading advocates of the utilitarian philosophy was Jon Stuart Mill, who said that anything was good which gave pleasure for the greatest number.

Aristotle, on the other hand, felt that virtue depended upon the possession and exercise of intelligence as a guide of behaviour. To him virtue laid between the two extremes of bad and good. For John Locke (1650) values were the product of experience. He believed that circumstances made things good or bad, right or wrong. However, Kant disagreed and said that right was known as a priori and was independent of circumstances. He spoke of a 'categorical imperative' by which he meant a moral command that must be obeyed by everybody.

Bertrand Russell reflected that values were simply emotional attitudes which could be proved true or false. He argued that to attribute universally to good was merely an attempt to universalize personal attitudes. Freud (1900) said that ideas of good and bad came from the super ego which was part of the personality. It developed in childhood, and was composed of the ego-ideal (formed by what parents considered good) and conscience (formed by what parents disapproved of)

Religions generally hold the view that an action is good if it is in accordance with the will of the Deity. God, according to St. Augustine, is the *summun bonum* (the highest good) of man. St. Thomas and Aristotle felt the goal of all creation was good, and could be achieved by the performance of its proper activity. They said that what was good should please God. Man's activity must therefore be geared to attaining the *summun bonum* i.e. (God)

Is Education Good?

The philosophy of humanism is optimistic about the future of man, and it feels that education can accelerate the process of evolution towards a happier future for man. It concerns itself with human matters. Humanism believes in fostering science rather than classics. It must, however, be noted that initially the study of classics was encouraged so that the original source of Aristotle's science could be studied. Humanism is human and against cruelty. It is anti-authoritarian and consequently favours the secularization of education. It abhors punishment and respects the child's autonomous personality. Two of the earliest humanists were Pestalozzi and Froebel. They pioneered the kindergarten and non-formal education later on. Humanism is human in that as it feels that education should be concerned with human beings and not with supernatural problems. The highest morality of humanism is its recognition of human freedom.

While many people accept 'education is something good', they hold different views about who should receive education, and what type of education should different people receive. Some people advocate that education should be withheld from the majority on the grounds that only a few can benefit from it. This belief about education dates back from Plato who felt that different classes should have different education. He said that education should be based on religion, class, race, wealth, colour, political views, sex and the level of intelligence of the individuals. The danger with such a proposition is obvious to the national unity and also to peaceful coexistence.

On the other hand giving education to everybody to a high level is also too ideal. It is expensive and leads to the squandering of resources, the lowering of standards and a mass production of half-educated graduates. This leads to producing unemployed and embittered graduates. Mass unemployment in turn can cause a wave of crimes and a possible break down of law and order. In many countries unemployment of educated youths has led to a rural-urban population drift and its attendant problems of congestion and overburdening of amenities and utilities in towns and cities.

The idea of mass education is particularly rejected by the existentialists who also oppose science as a means of advancing the human race. They emphasize individuality and educating the individual for advancement. To them individual existence is more important rather than the collective will and commitment. Nietzsche and Kierkegaard are some of the names often associated with these views.

Education and the Common Good

There are different kinds of views in respect of providing education to the people. Some hold that in the modern society even one illiterate person can be harmful to the common good. Therefore the modern society largely presupposes education. In the same way advanced academic education for everybody can be harmful to the common good of society when a shortage of manual skills exists or when it creates mass unemployment among them. The common good also implies equal opportunity for all to attain education at any level. It is against discrimination in education. Therefore, to discriminate in education on any basis other than that of natural abilities is harmful to the common good. Such discrimination is against our sense of justice, which is based on the individual's right and his claim to participation in the common good.

Discrimination in education based on the alleged class inequalities has been common since Plato's time to the present day. These days there are occurrences of educational discrimination based on religion in a few countries. Whichever the case, educational discrimination based on religion, sex, race or any other social factor is harmful to the common good.

Sex discrimination is very ancient. It is possible that it would have originated from the muscular inferiority of women and reinforced by certain religious precepts in different societies. Many religions generally regard women as inferior. Freudian psychologists regard them as feeling incomplete. In Switzerland women did not have a right to vote until 1971. In many countries they do not pay taxes and in many others, including the Soviet Union, they earn less salary than men, and are expected to retire from their job/s professions before the prescribed age for men. In all cases when resources and jobs are scarce it appears to be less reasonable to neglect women's education. Since men are the only bread winners and if they are assisted by the women in that respect, it would be a great benefit to the family and to the society as well.

However, the U.S.S.R. has proved that women are equally competent at most jobs, and they are no longer expected to remain at home. The common good therefore, demands education for women too. We must not lose sight of the fact that if we educate a man we educate an individual. To educate a nation we have to educate women.

Co-education is a modern concept, pioneered in the U.S.A. It is not yet accepted at secondary level in many undeveloped countries. Many reasons are advanced for its non-acceptance. Some people say that each sex needs a different curriculum, and that sex related problems arise particularly among adolescents attending a co-educational institution. Against these, it is argued that society is not mono-sexual, and school should reflect what is natural. Problems militating against co-education are more acute in boarding institutions, but the trend now is towards day schools. It is hoped that the day school system will facilitate the acceptance of co-education.

The Good Curriculum

Naturalists like pragmatists emphasize the utility criterion of the good curriculum. They say that the school's responsibility is to enable the child to store enough experience so that he can lead a worthwhile life. Their criterion is that the curriculum must include knowledge and skills that the child requires for future life. According to Aristotle children should be taught those useful things which are really necessary. They should be assisted to develop the habits, skills, interests and sentiments which they would need for their community. Dewey emphasizes that the child should always be considered as the centrepiece of a good curriculum. He stresses that to prepare the child for his future he must have a rich and full experience. His education should be based on his natural activities and interests.

In Sparta a 'good curriculum' was to produce good soldiers. Physical training was, therefore, all that was important to the Spartans. Emphasis on the physical aspect of education, particularly as a means of producing soldiers, was also in evidence in most of the ancient Greece. It reappeared in nineteenth century in Britain in the guise of character training when the now defunct Empire was expanding. Since that time physical training in education has occupied an important place in the educational system at all levels, particularly in the curriculum of the boarding schools.

The Greeks felt that the curriculum should educate the whole man—his mind, soul and body. It should provide a balanced education, which in turn should produce a good individual and a good citizen. They also emphasized the importance of physical, mental and spiritual training of the child so that he could become a balanced human being. The proverb that a healthy mind is found in a healthy body emphasizes the need for both physical and mental fitness derived from a balanced curriculum.

In most countries of the world the debate has always hinged on who should control education. Some people say it is only the government that can establish a public system of education that can protect a 'good curriculum'. Others are not convinced of the dangers, if any, of denominational schools. Yet others advocate government aid to denominational schools on the grounds that these schools do the job which the state would otherwise bear. People who possess different views say that no aid should be given to denominational schools because they cause sectarian divisions. Nevertheless, both sides seem to agree that religious education is necessary to maintain civilization, moral standards and discipline in society.

The Sophists in Plato's time were despised because their curriculum included vocational training. Aristotle advocated a similar curriculum when he said that in addition to learning his own language, the child should be taught history and geography so that he as a citizen could understand the problems of everyday life. He added that, depending on what life the child would lead, he should be taught agricultural science and domestic science if the child is a girl. He recommended vocational training for the child at a later stage. Nowadays, vocational training is the most important element that has been included in the school curriculum at the school level in most countries of the world. The emphasis these days is laid on making the child a maker, a creator and a doer. A good curriculum, it is believed, centres around the child, making him discover knowledge and become creative. Thus, Dewey advocates that work in school should consist of activities.

The Good Pupil

There are several views on 'who is a good student?' Authoritarians enforce orders and discipline on the pupil. Authority, according to them, must be obeyed. They say that the good student does what he is told and that the person in authority is always right. This type of authoritarian attitude is based on religion, class, race, tradition or pride. It is the attitude traditionally adopted towards the pupil.

On the other hand, naturalism is opposed to authoritarianism. Rousseau said that the pupil should not be given verbal orders but be taught by experience alone. He advocated that the pupil should learn natural behaviour because human institutions are one mass of folly and contradictions. He said that the pupil should be left to decide his own field and direction in that respect. Many people these days share Rousseau's views. This school of thought advocates that de-schooling and informal education is often superior to formal schooling.

The Good Teacher

Traditionally the teacher was expected to stand in *loco parentis*. Parents expected strict discipline, a reinforcement of parental attitudes, and a filling of the mind with facts. Nowadays it is recognized that a teacher has to prepare pupils, not only for life within the family, but also as citizens. However, a good teacher ensures that his methods of instructions, of disciplining and of indoctrination, are not opposite to parental wishes and for the common good. Nowadays, academic freedom is tolerated if it does not challenge the basic philosophical position of society. In that respect the teacher's role is not only difficult but greatly challenging, highly pragmatic as well as yielding good in all respects.

The Good School

Traditionally, a good school was the one which got good examination results and had strict discipline. Today it is realized that examinations and qualifications may not necessarily be leading to providing good education and branding a school good. Our ideas relating to disciplining children have also changed. This is mainly due to the naturalist's influence on education. Silence and order are no longer considered essential to discipline, neither is a school in which silence and order are practised, regarded as good. A good school now generally believes in an impressionistic approach and strikes a balance between repression-ism and naturalism. Harsh punishment is muted and is replaced by the idea of reforming the pupil by exposing him to better situations so that he may grow as a complete human being. The idea of retribution is basically sadistic and meant only to satisfy over anxious administrators. Therefore, nowadays a good school is one which takes care to reform pupils by discovering a variety of ways and methods to exploit his hidden talents. That would also help him grow as good citizens in future.

Questions

1. What is the meaning of good according to Socrates?
2. The highest morality of humanism is its recognition of freedom: Discuss.
3. How can education lead to the common good? Discuss.
4. What kind of curriculum you think would be considered good for the benefit of the pupil? Discuss briefly.

Chapter Four

Naturalism in Education

Historical Perspective

Naturalism may be described as a modified form of materialism. However, unlike materialism, naturalism does not hold that all things consist of matter and whatever exists can be satisfactorily explained in natural or scientific terms.

Historically, the earliest exponent of naturalistic views was the Greek philosopher, Thales, who lived in the 6th Century B.C., Thales confined himself to the study of nature which he believed, held the key to knowledge of the ultimate reality. It was not until the 17th century that the interest in naturalistic interpretations of the world came to light again, and this was due largely to the philosophy of Thomas Hobbes. According to Hobbes, philosophy is 'natural' and is mainly concerned with the properties of bodies. Following Hobbes, Herbert Spencer translated some of the new scientific ideas of the period into a philosophy of education in the form of 'scientific naturalism'.

A leading inspiration of the new movement was the philosopher, Rousseau, who was a prime example of the attitude of protest which was characteristic of both, the enlightenment period during which Rousseau was writing, and also of the spirit of naturalistic philosophy. Rousseau, who is often referred to as the father of modern progressive education, spent his life criticising the established institution of his day.

In his famous educational treatise *Emile*, he reflected: 'Reverse the usual practice and you will almost always do right. As a naturalist, he was totally opposed to any form of institutionalised learning. Human institutions were, for Rousseau, one mass of folly and contradiction.

The appearance and reappearance of naturalism, after the 17th century, coincided with times of social and intellectual unrest and can be seen as part of a reaction against the existing order of things.

During the 18th century, naturalism was revived in order to combat Humanism which by this time had degenerated into confusion and sterility. Following the First World War, social conditions led to a weakening of the pioneering favour which had inspired the 19th century educational reformers, and it was against this background that naturalistic ideas found a new lease of life.

The criticism of social institutions to which naturalism concentrated has had far reaching effects on the development of educational theory and practice.

Types of Naturalism

There are three types of naturalism. First, there is the Naturalism of the Physical Sciences, which holds the notion that the universe is composed entirely of matter. Everything in it including the mind is matter and there is no spirit or soul. Matter which is made up to atoms, empty space and motion, keeps on changing through motion, governed by the laws of nature explained by the physical sciences. Man is a complex combination of atoms. According to this theory, he has no soul or creative force, and no ultimate purpose or direction.

This kind of naturalism or materialism has had little impact on educational theory because it fixes its attention merely on phenomenon and failed to provide any satisfactory account of man.

A second form of naturalism is Mechanicalism attributed to Hobbes and inspired by Galileo, which explains the universe in terms of a large and complex machine and asserts that human behaviour is also explicable in terms of such a model. Man's behaviour is causal and governed by mechanical laws. His thoughts, life and purpose are completely internal and can be fully understood in terms of the psychological notions of conditioning and stimulus-response theory. This form of naturalism provides the basis for many of the ideas of behaviourist psychology, pioneered by the American B.F. Skinner, which continues to exert considerable influence on certain spheres of educational practice.

A third type of naturalistic philosophy, Biological Naturalism is based upon the theory of evolution and seeks to explain man in terms of lower animals. According to Russell, "Man has developed out of the animals and there is no serious gap between him and amoeba". This leads to the conception of man as simply a sophisticated animal. He is the 'result of the action of his environment in accordance with the laws of natural selection. These laws can explain his environment, so they can also explain him.'

By this account, real man is nothing more than the collection of natural impulses which man has in common with the animals. Ross summarises this position well in his observation:

Natural impulses are therefore of great importance and are regarded as good in themselves. Nature, in the sense of man's instincts, primitive emotions, and unsophisticated judgements, is held to be a more trustworthy and reliable guide to conduct, than reflections or the capitalized results of experience.

Naturalism and Education

(i) No Institutional Education

According to John Adams, naturalism is a term which is loosely applied to systems of training which are not dependent upon schools and books. Naturalistic educators prefer to start from the actual life of pupils and to utilize this in bringing pupils back to nature. All training and education must be in keeping with the natural development of the child.

Rousseau, for instance, was appalled by the formal schooling practices of his time. Education for the pupil Emile was to proceed according to nature. "Our foolish and pedantic methods", he wrote, "are always preventing children from learning what they could learn much better by themselves." Emile was, therefore, to be taken away from his parents, away from society and school and to be educated by an ideal tutor in close and direct contact with nature. The child's whole environment is the book from which he unconsciously enriches his memory.

(ii) Happiness as an Aim of Education

Rousseau's educational philosophy has had far-reaching and lasting impact on educational thought and planning, and the central claims of naturalism continue to arouse controversy. If natural impulses are considered as being good in themselves in that they are conductive to human pleasure, then this obviously has important implications for education. The central aim becomes the promotion of present and future happiness in pupils, and this clearly alters the structure and purpose of schooling.

This notion of human happiness was central feature of the philosophical utilitarianism of the 19th century and it continued to exert influence on the ideas of educators and philosophers.

(iii) Adjustment to the Environment

Naturalism stresses the idea of man's evolution from lower forms of life. Thus, educational aims based upon such notions will refer to the selective action of the environment on man, along with the struggle for existence and the survival of the fittest. The aim of enabling pupils to adjust to their environment will, therefore, become an important feature of curriculum. As Ross describes:

Education is seen as the process of adjustment to environment; it aims at enabling the individual to be in harmony with well-adopted surroundings.

(iv) Importance of the Child's Nature

Keeping in view the importance of the child-centred education, naturalistic educators emphasise the 'innate nature of the child'. Education, on this view, should provide only such experiences as will help to channel the development of pupils in a direction dictated by their natures. Educators accepting this position are more interested in the child as he is, rather than as he will be. Exalted adult standards are, therefore, of little importance to him. Education is not merely a preparation for living but living itself; and childhood is regarded as a desirable and valuable state in itself. In Rousseau's words, 'Nature would have them children before they are men'. Rousseau thus envisages the development of a natural life for children through the provision of experiences designed to foster the growth of a balanced and harmonious personality.

For Rousseau and his followers, true education takes place 'when the nature, powers and inclinations of the child are allowed to develop freely with a minimum of guidance. Naturalistic educators favour methods which allow pupils to follow their interests with a minimum of external interference. Adult manipulation of the child's natural development is seen as antithetical to genuine education.

(v) The Role of the Teacher

Radical exponents of naturalism in education eschew completely the role of institutionalised schooling. However, accepting the existence of mass formalised schooling as a given fact, the task for educators can become constructive by providing an ideal environment for the natural development of pupil.

The teacher's role is that of observer and guide, rather than authoritarian instructor or law giver. He sets the stage and creates the environment within which natural development can be fostered. Montessori, for instance, pioneered the use of apparatus in the classroom especially designed to encourage experimentation in children's learning. The Montessori teacher was a 'directress' who, through the skilful use of the 'sense training apparatus', was to lead pupils naturally 'from the abstract, to the association of ideas.

We may sum up the naturalistic concept of teaching by saying that it is the child himself, rather than the educator or school, who is the chief agent of learning. The teacher assists in the learning process through his knowledge of child development and the psychology of intellectual progress. His approval and guidance, combined with the pupil's natural curiosity to understand the world facilitate the kind of development favoured by naturalists.

(vi) Direct Experience as a Means of Learning

Direct experience is the chief method employed in naturalistic education. Realism supports this naturalistic trend which lays stress on experience with concrete objects rather than verbal instructions. For instance, science should not be taught solely from text-books and lectures but learned by the pupil through practical work in laboratories. Concrete experience of the pupil's environment should be given primacy. Similarly, geometry can be learned more effectively through the application of rules and concepts to practical tasks such as estimating the areas of playgrounds and fields. Geography should make abundant use of field trips and excursions, and the learning of language will take place against the background or practical and functional conversation. Thus, the chief emphasis is placed on direct experience. The pupil is educated in the intellectual and social sphere through practical learning situations which link the school environment to the wider community of which the school sis an integral part.

(vii) The Play Way

Psychological studies have demonstrated the importance of play in the development of child. Naturalists assert that play, rather than being wasteful activity, is the means by which the creative spirit of man is expressed. Creativity and play methods, therefore, are given a special emphasis in naturalistic education.

Both Montessori and Froebel made extensive use of such methods and designed various pieces of apparatus by which children could learn through play. For Froebel, play was the 'highest phase of child-development'. In a similar vein, Coldwell Cook, one of the greatest proponents of the play-way method, maintained that the play spirit went 'far deeper than study' passing 'beyond reasoning'. But in addition to the quality of love, leadership, freedom and self-discipline which are associated with play; naturalistic educators place so high a value on the play-way method that they consider it a means to natural development of the child.

Influence of Naturalistic Education

Various aspects of naturalism have influenced the development and planning of modern education round the world. Naturalistic educators place emphasis on practical, direct experience in teaching-learning process and this philosophy can be discerned in school practice.

The bookish type of education, a remnant of the missionary influence, is severely criticised. The aim of education is not to produce clerks and shopkeepers but skilful men who can fulfil the manpower needs of a modern technological nation. This stress on practical objectives and concrete experience is fully in keeping with the tenets of naturalistic education.

The majority of people are farmers in our country and they are dependent upon agricultural products to sustain its economy. Because of the importance of farming in our community, it is not out of place to state the relation between primary education and agriculture. If the schools are not to be entirely divorced from the life and work of the people, they must see to it that the work that goes on in the classroom draws meaning and colour from the activities of the community. Naibi, a Hungarian educationist holds that, "some practical work concerned with the cultivation of the land, the growing of crops, and the care of livestock should certainly have a place in the school curriculum. "

Similarly, in addition to academic training, pupils need to be taught skills and crafts, such as leatherwork, weaving, basketwork, mat weaving and fishing. More modern skills such as carpentry and brick-making also need to enter the curriculum of primary and secondary schools. One of the key objectives and slogans of contemporary education is effective citizenship, and to this end the new subject of social studies need to be strengthened at the secondary school and S T C levels. The aim of such courses is to enable the pupil to learn something about the right and responsibility of a good citizen.

All these educational aims and innovations contain some of the basic tenets of Naturalistic education. Primary school teaching methods also reveal the influence of Montessori's and Froebel's ideas in their stress on activity learning so that a broad range of knowledge in addition to the 3 Rs may be acquired by pupils. In primary schools, learning should no longer be a passive activity but a dynamic active, utilizing play-way method and direct experience. Besides, the teacher's stern eye needs to be replaced by a caring conduct in which punishment is very seldom used to enforce discipline.

Questions:

1. Describe the three main types of naturalism.
2. List some of the main influences of naturalistic philosophy on educational theory and practice.
3. What naturalistic ideas are reflected in the organization, planning and objectives of the educational system of the modern India?

assembly under the guidance [illegible] Ashoka, which took place in 247 [illegible] teachings of Buddha were collected together [illegible] these teachings into three parts, called [illegible] Pitaka and *Abhidhamma Pitaka*, which [illegible] Buddhist literature. But the sects established [illegible] interpret his teachings according to their own whims which led to the division of the Buddhist sect into two groups—[illegible] and the Hinayana.

[illegible] school of Indian philosophy that has been most popular among [illegible] is the philosophy of Buddha. Buddha [illegible] popularised *upanishadic* thought though [illegible] form. [illegible] stand this change of form, one must understand [illegible] prevailing in that period. It is known [illegible] that in Buddha's time and before him, [illegible] other world, sins and liberation etc. [illegible] the country was divided into [illegible] inhabitants used different languages [illegible] till then assumed [illegible] sacred in the spiritual [illegible] more importance than [illegible] depended on [illegible] the sense of responsibility [illegible] everywhere superstition [illegible] became common. [illegible] presented a rational religion [illegible] that follow here under.

Chapter Five

Idealism in Education

Introduction

As a philosophical term, Idealism refers to any view which emphasises the central role of the ideal or the spiritual in man's interpretation of his experiences. It can be taken to mean that reality exists mainly as spirit and that abstraction and laws are more fundamental to our knowledge of reality than sense perceptions. Whatever exists is known to man through mind or ideas.

Idealism is thus directly opposed to materialism, the view that matter is the basic substance of the world, and it is also opposed to realism, which holds that in human knowledge objects are seen and known as they really are. According to idealism, nothing is known outside and independently of the mind.

The essential features of idealism can be understood through some of its typical tenets: 'Truth is the whole, or the Absolute'; 'To be is to be perceived'; 'Reality reveals its ultimate nature more faithfully in its highest qualities (mental) than its lowest (material)'; 'The Ego is both subjective and objective'. Great stress is laid by idealists on supernatural or transcendental ideas. Plato says that beyond this world and this life, there is another world or life more real, true, beautiful and eternal which we can know through our reason. This eternal world provides us with the moral standards to follow; thus, morality, truth and justice and righteousness are not matters of expediency, changing their form time to time, but external and permanent features of reality. However, ordinary sense experience can only reveal the various objects of the world, but behind these lie the external ideas or forms which can be grasped only through the mind.

A Historical View

In the Western world, idealism began with Socrates when he discussed problems with Parmenides, Pythagoras and other early Greek thinkers. Socrates' disciple, Plato, believed that there are Ideas or Forms (see Unit 3, section of Metaphysics) which are real and lasting and compared with which the objects of the senses are transitory and imperfect. Plato's 'allegory of the cave' in *The Republic* unfolds the theme that the world of the senses, is a shadowy world, and that in order to know pure ideas one needs to withdraw from sense experiences and rely on pure intellect. Ross sums up this position in his statement that:

> *Idealist philosophy takes many tarried forms but the postulate underlying all is that mind and spirit is the essential world-stuff; that true reality is of a mental character.*

During the 4th century, St. Augustine in his *Demagistro*—an inquiry into the origin of ideas continued his reflections on idealistic tradition. The modern beginning of idealistic revival came after the Renaissance. The French thinker, Rev. Descarte, reflected that self was the prime reality and the existence of God was necessary. Spinoza believed that there existed eternally a substance in the world which is named God. Leibniz thought that there were simple indivisible entities which made up the cosmos. He called these entities Monads which he reclaimed as points of mental force.

The idealistic tradition was further continued and developed by George Berkeley, Immanuel Kant and Hegel. In fact, the idealistic movement reached its pinnacle with Hegel and Arthur Schopenhauer. Hegel conceived that the phenomenal world has a manifestation of infinite mind and the so called physical world was simply an idea. The German philosopher, Schopenhauer considered that the world was merely a conception of man's will. Schopenhauer greatly influenced the English, French and American philosophers who came after him.

However, there are various forms of idealism underlying this common principle and it is necessary to distinguish the main stands of the philosophy which have been proposed over the centuries.

The Types of Idealism

(a) Subjective Idealism

Both Leibnitz and Berkeley were 'subjective' idealists who conceived reality in terms of the experiences of the individual mind.

Leibnitz argued that true atoms of nature were 'monads' or 'souls' and that, in the last analysis, nothing existed in the world apart from minds. Berkeley adopted a position with reduced reality to spirit (his name for subjects) and the ideas entertained by spirits. He was extremely subjective in his approach and, in his version of idealism; the apparent objectivity of the world outside the self was explained by the claim that its objects are ideas of the mind of God.

(b) Objective Idealism

Immanuel Kant, the founder of 'objective idealism' in the late 18th century, presented a formalistic or transcendental introspection of the main idealist themes. Kant thought that the human self, or 'transcendental ego', constructs knowledge out of sense impressions upon which are laid universal concepts which were labelled categories.

In the early 19th century, Hegel, inspired by this Kantian interpretation, put forward the idea that the human world was made up of mind-made objects in that it consisted of a series of structures, examples would be languages and practical art such as medicine, which constituted mental achievements.

The world of nature for Hegel was in one sense independent of the mind but was relevant to the mind in that it provided a setting in which the mind could act and construct obstacles which it could overcome. In reply to the question of why there was a world of nature at all, Hegel's only answer would be 'for the sake of mind'. Man transforms the natural scene and makes it his own. Thus, Hegel's account of the world as it is, is no far from Kant's account for whom self constructs knowledge of the world out of sense impressions structured by universal category systems

(c) Scientific Idealism

Neo-Kantian or Scientific Idealism founded by Hermann Cohen applied Kant's critical methods to humanistic and scientific studies as well. This school of thought underwent a remarkable development under the leadership of Cassirer who was noted for his clear analysis of man defined as a creator of culture through a unique capacity for symbolic representation. This kind of idealism has been extremely influential in shaping Russian culture and society.

(d) Theistic Idealism

Theistic Idealism was founded by R.H. Lotze, who propounded the theory of the 'world ground' in which all phenomena find their unity. According to this view, the world ground is the transcendental synthesis of evolutionary world process which is both mechanical and teleological (purposive).

T. H. Green and F. H. Bradley are Lotze's followers and their metaphysical writings place them firmly in the sphere of theistic idealism. This school of thought received classic arguments for the existence of God and used recent advances in the physical, biological and behavioural science to support their views. The cosmological proof of God's existence was restated as the continuing relation of the cosmos to a world ground that is spiritual in essence.

Idealism and Education

A wide influence of idealism on education can be seen in various directions. The important issue of education which have greatly been influenced by the philosophy of idealism are follows:

(i) The Ideal of Free-Will and the Importance of Human Personality

Idealism considers the world of experience more important than the external world. It insists that man, the experiencer, is of paramount importance and that the human personality should be accorded the highest value. Man is endowed with rationality and, thus, is able to choose his actions freely. As a free agent, in consciousness of this liberty, the spirituality of his soul is displayed and he may resist the base impulses of human nature. Idealism thus stands opposed to determinism and confirms that man, as a free agent, can choose and decide between right and wrong actions. Kant's view was that the exercise of reason necessarily leads us to the notion of duty and that duty in its turn is rooted in freedom.

The idea of freewill is one of the most important influences of idealistic philosophy on educational thought. The educational ideas of Froebel, one of the early progressive educators, were influenced by aspects of this philosophy and the notions of 'freedom and self-determination'. The centrality of the pupil in the educational process, which still influences 'child-centred' educators to this day, is squarely in line with the idealist conception of the human personality.

(ii) Development of a Spiritual Man in a Spiritual Society

According to idealism, the origin and destiny of man are both divine. "Man is not simply an organism with flexible responses; he is self originating in a self." To achieve his divine destiny, man has to attain the perfection of his personality. Idealism contends that there is an inner harmony between the soul of man and the heart of the universe. For the idealist, "Man is essentially a spiritual being whose main aim in life must be to develop his spiritual nature."

Man's spiritual nature is both individual and social. Perfection may be attained by him when he is a member of a group since personality requires a social medium to grow and flourish. Now the universe, like man, is also moving towards a divine goal. Thus, both man and the universe, being spiritual by nature, strive to attain the self-realisation which is the ultimate goal. To help man to attain this goal, therefore, society must be organised in accordance with certain spiritual and moral principles. Education is thus central to the idealistic enterprise of helping man to build his character and enabling him to achieve knowledge of God and self-realisation. These twin notions of character development and self-realisation have influenced education since the centuries.

(iii) The Importance of the Teacher

The teacher is accorded a central role in the idealist conception of education. He is the personification of reality and is expected to display professional excellence in all his activities. The teacher's role in helping his pupils to reach their goal in life cannot be over emphasised. The idealist teacher will constantly seek to promote maturity in his pupils and help them to attain self-realisation. He will always be conscious of his ultimate goal and will deliberately motivate pupils to move in that direction.

The teacher's principal contribution is, thus, to encourage and motivate growth and development in pupils in accordance with idealist perceptions. The pupil cannot turn into an infinite person without guidance. Thus, the teacher will organise activities designed to motivate pupils to search for the idealist conception of the good life. Thus good life is characterised by the eternal virtues of truth, beauty and goodness which are central to spirituality of man and in fostering the most important goals in systems of education from earliest times.

(iv) The Curriculum

The curriculum in an idealistic school should be structured by the liberal conception of education which favours a grounding in all the disciplines – the sciences and the arts. These areas of study will expose learners to all what is noble, generous and faith-inspiring in human knowledge and achievement.

However, following Rousseau and the Naturalists, Idealists, do not limit the educational task to the study of books. Direct experience of objects and places must complement classroom work. Following the *dictum* that nature is the book out of which pupils learn, teachers will encourage first-hand observation of natural phenomena, and will attempt to stimulate creativity by linking work in language and Arts with field trips and excursions. The Socratic method of questioning and discussion will, similarly, supplement this general approach to education by promoting self-reflection and an enquiring attitude on the part of pupils to help in the achievement of the central idealist goal.

(v) The Impact of Idealism on Education

Idealism, as a school of philosophy has influenced educational thinking about the curriculum, teaching methods and the school environment in many countries, and its influenced can be traced in determining the educational objectives of the developing countries of the world. The freedom of the pupil and the development of his character and personality are being given increasing attention in most of the Third World countries. In addition, curriculum objectives are now beginning to reflect the notions of creativity and self-realisation which are the hallmark of idealism.

The respect for worth and dignity of the individual, the fostering of 'moral and spiritual values in interpersonal and human relations', and the 'promotion of the emotional, physical and psychological health of the children', are all mentioned as values which the education system of all the countries should positively emphasize. Thus we may say that the influence the Idealism on education has been and continues to be wide-ranging and pervasive.

Questions:

1. What are the main features of idealistic philosophy?
2. How may idealism be said to have influenced ideas on curriculum and teaching?
3. Discuss the connection between idealistic principles and curriculum objectives at the secondary school level in our country.

Chapter Six

Realism in Education

A Brief Historical View

Like naturalism and idealism, the roots of realism can be located in the times of the ancient Greeks. Aristotle can be said to be the first realist for it was he who first brought the notion that nature is the only proper starting point of philosophers.

St. Thomas Aquinas reasserted the importance of realism in medieval times maintaining that 'God created Matter, although out of nothing.' During the 17th century, Comenius conceived of the idea of man's mind as 'a mirror which projects the impressions of the external world', whereas Descartes held that 'the reality of the physical world can be experienced by the senses'. Locke later contributed to the tradition through his assertion that the 'primary qualities of experience are contained in the physical world'. Locke's philosophy rejected the notion of the existence of 'innate ideas' which structure our perception of the world. For him, 'the child's mind at birth is like a blank sheet of paper', and it is the blank sheet or *tabula rasa* which gathers the impressions of the external world.

The realist tradition was further extended and supplemented by the work of philosophers such as Kant, Herbert and James who viewed the external world as a real phenomenon and regarded mind, or the knower of this phenomenon, as a witness of the representation of the external objects.

What is Realism?

The doctrine of realism is that there is a 'real world of things behind and corresponding to the objects of our perception'. Russell referred to this doctrine as a 'scientific philosophy' in that it consisted of a logical analytic approach to the problems of reality, existence and perception. 'Realism believes that reality exists independently of the mind and is confined to what we know with our sensations'. In a similar vein, Rusk refers to the aspect of realism which 'ignores the higher mental activities and the wider experience which transcends sensory perceptions. It is through sensory perceptions that the realists seek the real.

Thus, the realist philosophy is essentially contained in the idea that the universe consists of real entities. The objects of our perception have a 'reality independent of mental phenomena.'

Types of Realism

There are three main types of realism:

(i) Scholastic Realism

In medieval times realists argued, in opposition to the nominalists, that universals (i.e. properties or qualities predicted of all the individuals of a class of objects) have a real existence and substance independently of being thought. Further it was held that reason was capable of being thought. Further it was held that reason was capable of reaching the most sublime truths of the natural order and that even supernatural truths were capable of being comprehended by the human mind.

(ii) Naturalist Realism

This doctrine asserts that the external world, existing independently of mind, is governed by natural laws. The human mind has a biological origin and can be concerned as an instrument for adjustment to external forces in the world. On this view, man is bestowed with intelligence which he utilizes in his struggle against external nature.

(iii) Scientific Realism

It is also known as empirical realism. This approach stresses the idea that objects have a definite, physical existence. In Kant's words: 'All outer perception, therefore, yields immediate proof of something real in space, or rather is the real itself. In this sense, empirical realism is beyond question'. Physical objects, therefore exist externally to man's mind, and the laws which govern changes in the external world have to be discussed by scientific investigation.

Realism and Education

The influence of realistic philosophy can be discerned in a number of areas of educational theory and practice.

(a) The School and Practical Training

From the point of view of realism, it is desirable that curriculum activities reflect the life and culture of the wider community of which the school is a part. Strong links between school and community should be established, and the school be regarded as an important means of giving practical training in citizenship.

(b) The School Curriculum Reflects the Past and Present

A realist would wish to reframe various subjects of the school curriculum so that they reflect certain relevant aspects of society's past and present.

In the teaching of history, present events will be understood and interpreted in the light of the past, and this knowledge may also be utilized in the important area of civics. Mathematics must aim 'primarily at an understanding of the world in its numerical and spatial aspects'. In a similar way, the teaching of science must emphasise the practical, technological applications of scientific research and study so that the subject does not degenerate into a formal unreality. In summary, all special studies in school should keep closely in touch with those aspects of the outside world of which they are reflection.

(c) Vocational Education

This aspect of education is accorded a special status in a realist programme. Bearing in mind individual differences in intelligence, aptitude and interests of pupils, preparation for a future career is regarded as a central educational objective. Information of all spheres and types of vocational training and careers will be called upon in the promotion of this important aim, and this particular emphasis can be seen reflected in the establishment of special vocational institutions and polytechnics in developing and underdeveloped countries around the world.

(d) Cultural Education

In spite of the significance accorded to vocational training, realists also insist that education has a strong cultural or liberal component. Preparation for life in society, after all, must take account of an individual's needs for participation in cultural and leisure activities in addition to the more specific career and professional training. There is often an imbalance between the vocational and cultural sides of a school's curriculum with the result that the education offered is either too technical or too academic. In a realists programme, however, the liberal and vocational elements must be given equal emphasis.

(e) Utility Criterion

Realism stresses the utility foundation of the educational enterprise, the notion that education in any sphere has its ultimate – aims at the promotion of growth, progress and health of a community. Locke prescribed for the youth of the society a kind of education which would not only train them to become useful and civilized citizens, but also equip them for a particular vocation or profession. Knowledge, skills and curriculum activities in general therefore, will be selected on the basis of utility criterion.

The Impact of Realism on Education

The influence of certain themes in realist philosophy can be discerned in a number of areas in educational system of many countries in Africa & Asia.

The construction of diversified courses and curricula recommended by adherents of realism has become a common practice in many Third World Countries. This type of course organization enables pupils to choose subjects in which they are interested in addition to following those courses necessary for their future careers. Similarly, the stress on 'technical education' is reflected in the aims of modern education and in the rapid growth of polytechnics and vocational institutions.

The emphasis on citizenship training and on the importance of the socialization function of education is squarely in line with the realist perspective.

Similarly, the practical and functional themes of realist education are reflected in a number of contemporary aspects of our country. In response to the expectations that education should aim at 'effective citizenship and civic responsibility', and help promote education for 'national unity' and 'scientific and technological rareness', subjects like Social Studies and General Science have been introduced into secondary school curricula.

In language, teaching instruction in the mother tongue has been introduced into primary schools. At the secondary level, the curriculum and subject-content, especially in the areas of History, Education and Social Studies, reflect the national themes and objectives with special emphasis being given to the functional and the practical. The realist philosophical perspective could not be more clearly expressed than in the National policy (1986) recommendations that the 'content of education must reflect the past, present and future of the dynamic Indian society.'

Questions

1. What are the main aspects of realistic education?
2. How far has the realistic movement influenced education in our country?
3. Trace the important changes brought to the curriculum at secondary school level in India through the influence of realism.

Chapter Seven

Pragmatism in Education

Historical Perspective

Though Pragmatism as a distinctive mode of philosophizing, is only as old as the 19th century, traces of pragmatic thinking can be discovered in the writings of the early Greek philosophers. The philosophers such as Heraclitus, Parmenides and Democritus, introduced empirical considerations into man's speculation about the world. Protagoras defined knowledge as sense perception and reflected in his famous *dictum of humo mensura,* that man is the measure of all things. During the 16th century, this mode of thought was re-emphasised in the form of Bacon's introduction of inductive logic as a scientific method. In the 19th century, Comte pioneered positivistic thinking, tracing the development of human thought from its theological and metaphysical stages to its positive stages.

Modern Pragmatism developed in late 19th century as a revolt against the sterile and useless metaphysics which dominated philosophy at that time. The main contributors to the philosophy are James Peirce, William James and John Dewey. They felt that theorising should have practical results and believed that their approach to knowledge and truth could be of tremendous utility in solving intellectual problems of all kinds and in forwarding social progress.

What is Pragmatism?

Pragmatism is essentially a method of solving or evaluating intellectual problems, and a theory about the sort of knowledge man is capable of acquiring. James stressed the 'cash value' of ideas and their utility in helping us solving problems and overcome difficulties. Theories, ideas and thinking itself were regarded as instruments to be used in practical business and solving the problems we experience.

The spirit of pragmatism is well expressed in Peirce's notion about the meaning of an idea. "To determine the meaning of an idea, put it into practice in the objective world of activities and whatever its consequences prove to be, these constitute the meaning of idea". Both Peirce and James opposed the traditional philosophical view that the truth of ideas is a property independent of human experience. Peirce asserted that 'if a thing works it is true'. James later gave this pragmatic interpretation a much wider application in philosophical circles. Both Peirce and James believe that the once an idea was tested in the world of affairs, its meaning could be depended upon. On other words, a certain permanency was attached to the outcome of the pragmatic test.

Dewey's contribution to pragmatism took the form of a modification and extension of these basic ideas. Peirce and James believed that ideas, once tested, had a degree of permanency but Dewey regarded truth as 'relativistic' and reflected that the 'universe was in a state of continual flux so there is no ultimate truth or reality'. Reality was born out of man's experience of the world and, thus, with changes in his experience on the world reality would also change.

Dewey applied these in his theory of instrumentalism or experimentalism which, because of its concern with human learning and knowledge, has been of particular interest to educators. On this view man is an experimenter and creator of values whose mental process can be seen as an adjustment to the stimuli of the environment. Thinking, for Dewey, arises out of problematic situations and man's reasoning, in this situation, follow a certain pattern.

(i) We are faced with a problem or a difficulty to overcome

(ii) This perplexity stimulates us to find out solutions to the problem.

(iii) These solutions are tested in practice.

(iv) Finally, one solution is seen to be most effective and this is adopted and memorised for future reference.

Thus, all learning can be seen as adoption of the organism to its environment by means of problem-solving.

In idealistic philosophy values are eternal and absolute but Pragmatism denies the existence of such fixed values. James, for instance, regarded our truths as man-made products' which possessed satisfactory results of our experience. He insisted that 'successful working and utility are the tests of the true, the good and all other values. Cash-value of truth can be seen in experimental terms only. Similarly, Dewey argued that morality was a social quality and that an individual could develop only through the social medium. The moral and the social quality of conduct, he noted, 'are in the last analysis, identical with each other'. Dewey thus insisted on the direction of thinking and theorising towards the solution of practical social problems and went on to link his philosophy with the democratic ideal in which individual members of society cooperate to realise the full potentialities of each, thus bringing about mutual progress and general social advancement.

Pragmatism and Education

Pragmatism, especially Dewey's interpretation of the basic philosophy, has been extremely influential in educational circles. Dewey is regarded as the 'father of progressive education' in America, and his ideas on problem solving and the links between education and social ideals have had an impact on educational thought throughout the world. The central ideas of experimental thinking and utilitarian values reflects the spirit of modern sciences and contemporary politics and, for this reason, the impact of Pragmatism has been far reaching. There are a number of areas in which the influence of Pragmatism on educational thought can be discerned.

(a) Democracy and Education

Emphasising the social aspect of educational pragmatism, Dewey reveals his faith in the values of democracy. He believed in democracy, not only as the best form of government, but also as a means of education. For him, democracy is 'more than a form of government. It is primarily 'a mode of associated living of conjoint communicated experience.' On this view, a democratic society is one that is better able to confront new situations, and try new solutions, since it does not have any rigid or preconceived ideology. It is, in essence, a form of social organization that is open to the exploration of new ways of meeting the difficulties, which man has to face. This is the ethos of the modern technological society, and the ideal can be seen embodied in documents such as the United Nations Charter.

(b) School, Societal and Individual Progress

The individual and society are inter-dependent; a better a fuller satisfaction of individual human needs means a healthier society. Pragmatism, therefore, stresses that schools pay serious attention to social objectives so as to foster the growth of harmonious and happy social community. The school must not simply concern itself with the transmission of society's inheritance of the past, but must also seek to acquaint pupils with knowledge of the society in which they are presently living. Thus, like the naturalists, pragmatic educators stress direct experience as a means of education and a process of learning. An informal school environment and strong links between the school and its surrounded community are regarded as essential. Dewey feared that if the aims of education were to become extrinsic, external to the process, individual growth and potentialities would be reduced. Thus, educational aims are regarded as intrinsic. As Dewey notes, 'the aim of education is to enable individuals to continue their education—the object and reward of learning is continued capacity of growth'.

The pragmatic emphasis on individual pupil-teacher contact, learning by experience and close school community links, are all designed to promote individual growth within the wider context of social progress.

(c) Learning by Doing

The pragmatic theory of knowledge and truth stresses the dynamic and active features of process of human learning. Thus, in the classroom the activity of learning is accorded greater significance than traditional instructions.

Following Dewey's notion of instrumentalism as the major feature is acquiring knowledge, pupils are presented with problematic situations out of which learning and knowledge arise. According to this view, the teacher is to guide and assist learning rather than merely offer traditional instruction. Moreover, activity, learning, and problem solving are linked with the democratic ideals, for a student trained in problem-solving will be able to be an active citizen of a democratic society, utilising his techniques for dealing with unresolved problems in co-operation with the larger social groups.

(d) Integration of Knowledge

Pragmatists criticise the traditional organization of knowledge on the basis of watertight compartments. Thus, the integration of learning activities rather than a curriculum grounded in separate subjects is a central feature of their approach to education. Adams, a British advocate of Dewey's methods, supported his approach and argued that we 'ought to abstain from dividing and parcelling out what nature has made one and indivisible'.

The idea is that learning, co-ordinated with general themes of topics, will provide the pupils with the necessary practical experience to handle the problems they will need to face in adult life. Although some scope must be allowed for specialisation in certain subject-areas at later stage of the educational system, the primary and early secondary levels can derive much benefit from the integrated approach to knowledge.

The basic conception is of a unified or holistic approach to knowledge. As Ross notes that, 'theoretically, a unifying principle is round in the rounded whole of human knowledge itself, including all the humanities and all the sciences'.

(e) The Project Method

The activity and problem solving approach to learning advocated by Dewey was responsible for the development of the 'project method' in education. It was first introduced by a disciple of Dewey, W.H. Kilpatrick in American schools in the 1920s to 1930s.

Kilpatrick did much to translate Dewey's pragmatism into practical classroom programmes and it was through his work that the philosophy was initially popularised. He advocated that learning should be 'essentially creative and dynamic befitting to the changing world. Like Dewey, he pointed to the interdependence of pupils in the modern world and suggested that pupils be encouraged to engage in community activities. "One thing the school can do, he argued, 'is to lay a foundation of social knowledge by having the pupils study their communities and undertake socially useful work along with others in the community'. Thus, practical projects not only enhance the growth of knowledge through problem solving, but also contribute to the promotion of democratic spirit in pupils.

Influence of Pragmatism on Education

Pragmatic philosophy has been influential in shaping educational policy in India in a number of important areas. First, the broad aims of education are concerned with 'social and political progress' and with 'national unity' and these are fully in line with pragmatic ideals. Towards this, improved training in basic agricultural sciences and practical agricultural techniques have been recommended at secondary school levels. Agricultural science is one of the important subjects added to the curriculum contents at college level. This is in line with the modern need of Indian society as well as pragmatic principles.

The developments in literacy and science teaching in recent years are clear illustrations of this approach. The diversification of the curriculum and the need to link school studies with community life are also prominent features of the Indian scene.

Finally, in general conception of the teaching/learning process and the purpose of education, the pragmatic tendencies may be clearly discerned. At the primary level, school should 'help individual to adapt and adjust to the changing society' and at the secondary stage, students should be able to think reflectively about national problems. Dewey's distaste for purely 'academic' is nowhere more strongly expressed in the educational objectives than in the National Policy 1986 recommendation that in Universities not only the traditional academic subjects should be taught, but the more pragmatic (professional/ vocational/ technical) course should also form part of university curriculum.

Thus, in the areas of curriculum, teaching/learning methods and general aims, pragmatism has exerted a considerable influence on the development of the Indian educational system.

Questions:

1. Trace the origins of pragmatism.
2. Describe Dewey's conception of instrumentalism in learning and acquisition of knowledge.
3. How is pragmatic ideal?
4. Explain how pragmatic thought has influenced the development of the national education system?

Chapter Eight

Existentialism in Education

A Historical View

There came a time when men began to wake up from the dream-like world of myth, with consciousness and developed critical thinking. It was this time that we find the existential themes coming up on the horizon. Karl Jaspers called this age the 'axial age' which could be dated around 500 B.C. It was also the time of the great Hebrew prophets from Amos and Jeremiah down to the time of prophets of the Exile. Greek culture had already flourished and their political institutions were developed. It was alongside all this that the scepticism and radical questioning of sophists made its appearance. It was the dawn of existentialism.

Existentialism can be regarded as a trend or theme in philosophy rather than a particular dogma or system. After the Sophists, its revival can be traced to the work of Kierkegaard at the beginning of the 19th century, but it was not until the 20th century that this philosophy became influential, largely as a result of the work of writers such as Heidegger, Jaspers, Marcel, Buber and Sartre.

Existentialism stands opposed to rationalist and empiricist doctrine that assume that the universe is a determined, ordered system intelligible to the reflective and contemplative observer. Instead,

Existentialists endorse a more subjective vision of reality; primacy is accorded to the existence of the individual, his presence and his participation in a constantly changing world.

Though united in the common theme reflecting the stress placed upon the individual existence and consciousness, existentialism constitutes a diverse group of philosophers. A religiously inspired theistic group, referred to as 'Personalists' by Curtis and Bourtwood, comprising of Marcel, Buber and Kierkegaard, turn for inspiration to Roman Catholic and Lutheran traditions. However, philosophers such as Heidegger and Sartre reject this religious tradition and propose 'atheistic' solutions to the predicament as they see it.

Basic Elements of Existentialism

(a) **Existentialist philosophy begins from man** himself rather than from nature. It is a philosophy which considers the subject of experience, the existent individual, the thinking self and his feelings more important in this world.

Each self-aware individual understands his own existence in terms of his own experience in the world. The self of which he is aware, is a thinking being, which has beliefs, hopes, fears and desires. No individual has a predetermined place in the scheme of things. Everyone is compelled to assume the responsibility of making choices in life of shaping his own identity. Sartre expressed this view pint in his famous dictum 'existence precedes essence'. He explains that this means that 'man first of all exists', encounters himself, surges up in the world and defines himself afterwards. If man, as existentialist sees him as not definable, it is because to begin with he is nothing. He will not be anything until later, when he makes something of himself.

(b) Many of the traditional problems of philosophy, for instance, the central themes of logic and epistemology, are paid little attention by existentialists who assert that the problem of being must take precedence over the problem of knowledge. Notions such as 'freedom', 'choice', 'responsibility' and 'decision' are considered to be more important than the traditional philosophic themes. The central problems of philosophy are those which are centred on the question of man's existence. As Macquarie notes, for existentialists, 'it is the exercise of freedom and the ability to shape the future that distinguishes man from all the other beings that we know on earth'. He further explains, 'The self as agent provides the central themes for existentialism, whereas traditional philosophy since the time of Descartes has concentrated attention on the self as subject, mainly the thinking subject. The problem of existence can have no significance if viewed partially or in abstraction. It can only be seen in terms of the impact that experiences make on a particular existent. Thus, the central experientialism can be described as the existent individual who is in quest of personal identity and selfhood.

(c) Stemming from his concern with man's existence and quest for identity are a number of familiar themes including finitude, guilt, despair and death. In their response to these facts of existence and pessimistic camps, depending upon their suggested solutions to the problems facing individuals, all writers of this ilk (camp) are aware of the tragic elements involved in existence. They realise that man's freedom and his potent desires (to find his 'personal being') meet with resistance and frustration, ending of course in, death, the negation of existence.

On the whole, it is the 'Personalist' philosophers such as Kierkegaard and Marcel who take the optimistic line and find in man's freedom the hope of personal triumph and salvation. For Buber, the primary problem for each individual is to rediscover what he calls the 'I-Thou' relationship the intimate interaction between man and man rather than man and the abstract world. He explains:

> *No system of ideas, no foreknowledge and no fancy intervene between I and Thou. The memory itself is transformed as it plunges out of its isolation into the unity of the whole. No aim, no lust, and no anticipation intervene between I and Thou. Desire itself is transformed as it plunges out of its frame into the appearance every means is an obstacle. Only when everything has collapsed does that meeting come about.*

Buber emphasises that although men are obliged to pass their lives in the 'I-It' world of objects, it is the 'I-Thou' world of human relations that they discover the meaning of life.

Sartre is typical of the pessimistic thinkers who, overcome by sense of the nothingness of life, can find little meaning or direction for mankind. According to Sartre, conscious beings, 'beings – for themselves' feel 'nausea' at the contemplation of the multiplicity and disorderliness of things and the world, and feel 'anguish' at the realisation of their own freedom. However, even the apparent pessimism of this philosophy does not degenerate into total despair, and it is here that the characteristic stress in the human psyche and emotions leads to the common existentialist plea for 'authenticity' of existence.

Faced with the anguish resulting from the full realisation of his freedom, a man may adopt a certain role or identity, solely in order to relieve these painful emotions. But this is an inauthentic response to freedom constituting what Sartre calls *Moutaise Foi*—Bad Faith. He cites as an example, the case of a waiter in a cafe who adopts certain mannerism in order to convince himself and others that he is just a waiter. But this is an inauthentic response which constitutes protection. Authenticity consists in recognising our capacity to make free choices in life and of realising that capacity. Significantly it is this aspect of existentialism, the quest for authenticity in behaviour, which has proved to be of great interest of educators and others concerned with the development of persons.

Existentialism and Education

At first look many of the key themes of existentialist philosophy – death, contingency, freedom and anxiety – may seem to be far removed from the concerns of educators. However, on closer inspection this concern with freedom of choice with authentic being and with the quest of selfhood can be seen to have considerable relevance for education. In the areas of teaching methods curriculum organization and overall educational objectives, a number, of significant existentialist influences can be discerned.

(i) Education and Human Development

Metaphysically existentialists believe that the world is devoid of all prior meaning; meaning is provided by human beings. Man, thus, defines himself, creates both what he is to be and in what relation he stands to the world around him. On this account, the task of an educator is to provide pupils with the wherewithal to define and shape themselves to find authentic personal identity within their relations with the world and with fellow humans. In Buber's terms, this involves the discovery of the 'I-Thou' relationship, and this discovery can be facilitated by the provision of suitable social context to schooling.

Addressing himself specifically to the question of the development of pupils, Morris expresses the existentialists, position in terms of general objectives of producing as individual who no longer needs to be taught, who breaks loose and swings free of the teacher and becomes self-moving. Thus, the educational enterprise ultimately succeeds by doing itself out of a job. In a similar vein, Barnes enumerates the three basic needs of pupils as the 'right to live the extreme choice', 'the right to change' and 'the right to spontaneous self-realisation'. Clearly, such applications of existentialists' values have radical implications for educational practice in general.

(ii) The Teacher's Role

Given their general views on human development, the question of pedagogic relationships and the teacher's role is naturally of the first importance to existentialist educators. Harper suggests that a good teacher is fully conscious of the fact that he is educating individuals: The aim of the teacher is to 'produce' not replicas, but men and women who stand apart from him more distinctly than when he first met them. The teacher takes full responsibility for the freedom of choice in his pupils. He is especially concerned with their emotional development and seeks to share the joys, sorrows, fears and delights of life with them. Above all, the teacher must attempt to foster the growth of authentic personalities in his pupils. Jeffreys sums up this objective when he argues that.

"...it is the teacher's obligation to combat everything that disintegrates human personality, undermines the value set upon persons as such, or reduces human life to abstractions. He must vigilantly reckon with all those influences in modern society which numb the sense of responsibility..."

The Curriculum

Given the general existentialist stand on freedom of choice, it is only to be expected that educators inspired by this philosophy, will be opposed to the traditional curriculum of rigid subject divisions which aims to mould pupils in terms of preconceived ideas of what constitutes an educated person. It is true, of course, that in order to become a free and responsible agent a pupil must in the first place have a group of various forms of understanding without which he could not properly function in society. In this context, White has argued that, without certain compulsory elements in a curriculum, the ideal of autonomy can never be fully realised. However, granted all this, the existentialist educator will strive to allow as much freedom of choice for pupils as possible in the curriculum. Primacy will be accorded, not to subject-matter, but to the pupil's reactions to subject-matter. As Prattle notes, 'Existentialists regard school subjects as tools for the realisation of subjectivity; knowledge exists only as it arises from human consciousness and feelings.'

Thus emphasis is placed upon the learner's role in the educational process. The curriculum must involve substantial elements; Morris expresses this view in extreme terms when he recommends the 'freest possible learning circumstances in schools. The development and the growth of authentic behaviour demand such learning conditions.

Impact of Existentialism Education

The influence of pragmatism and realism on Indian education has already been referred to in earlier chapters and in view of this, it may appear that existentialist thought has had little influence in this sphere.

Existentialism places a high value on individuality and freedom of choice and these values are found alongside and wider social values in Indian national curriculum objectives. The pursuit of 'self-realisation' for instance, is given prominence, as also is the respect for the worth and dignity of the individual. A broad and 'diversified' secondary school curriculum is also recommended and this is in keeping with existentialists' conception of human development. At the tertiary level, the pursuit of the 'goal of free inquiry after truth' recognises the fact that the growth of knowledge is dependent upon individual creativeness.

All these traces of existentialists' influence can be taken as an indication of the value placed upon individuals within the wider context of our pursuit of national unity and reconstruction. The experience of totalitarian states has shown us that a healthy and stable society cannot arise from mindless loyalty to mass values. A nation is a group of individuals whose collective health depends upon the health of each individual member. It is in its stress on individuality and self-hood that existentialism can make a contribution to the development of education in India.

Questions

1. What are the main tenets of existentialism?
2. Which themes are most popular with extentialists? Discuss.
3. How far the existentialist philosophy influenced the field of education?
4. What is the impact of existentialism on the Indian educational system?

SECTION C
ISLAM

Philosophy and Education

Before coming close to the aspects of education in relation to Islam, it is imperative to understand the basic tenets of Islam as without understanding its main principles it may be hard for some to appreciate how it has deep relationship with education.

Islam is the religion spoken by the *Qur'an*, a religious book, considered by its followers to be the verbatim word of the single incomparable God, and by the Prophet of Islam, Muhammad demonstrations and real-life examples (called the *Sunnat*, collected through narration of his companions in collections of *Hadith*). Islam literally means submission to God.

An adherent of Islam is a Muslim, meaning "one who submits (to God)". Muslims regard their religion as the completed and universal version of a monotheistic faith revealed at many times and places before, including, notably, to the prophets, Abraham, Moses and Jesus. Islamic tradition holds that previous messages and revelations have been changed and distorted over time. Religious practices include the Five Pillars of Islam, which are five duties that unite Muslims into one community. Islamic law reflects virtually on every aspect of life and society, covering everything from dietary laws, banking to warfare as well as defining appropriate conditions for war. The vast majority of Muslims belong to one of two major denominations, the Sunni and Shi'a. Islam is the predominant religion in the Middle East, North America, and a large part of Asia. Sizable Muslim communities are also found in China, Russia, Balkans, the Caribbean, Indonesia and Indian Subcontinent where the number of the community has reached almost 31 % of the whole population of Muslims in the world. Thus, Islam is the second-largest religion in the world and the fastest growing religion too.

The Meaning and Faith

The word Islam is derived from the Arabic verb Aslama, which means 'to accept, surrender or submit.' Thus, Islam means acceptance of and submission to God. The believers of Islam must demonstrate this by worshiping him, following his commands, and avoiding polytheism. There are a number of meanings of Islam in the Qur'an. In some verses, the quality of Islam is taken as an internal conviction: 'Whomsoever God desires to guide, He expands his breast to Islam.'

The *Qur'an* states that all Muslims must believe in God, his revelations, his angels, his messengers, and in the 'Day of Judgment'. The Sunni concept of predestination is called 'divine decree' while the Shi'a is called 'divine justice'. The *Qur'an* mentions the names of numerous figures considered prophets in Islam, including Adam, Noah, Abraham, Moses and Jesus among others. The *Qur'an* lists several sins that can condemn a person to hell, such as disbelief and dishonesty. Muslims view paradise (*jannat*) as a place of joy and bliss, with Qur'anic references describing its features and the physical pleasures to come. There are also references to a greater joy—acceptance by God. Mystical traditions in Islam place these heavenly delights in the context of an ecstatic awareness of God.

Free Will and Predestination

In accordance with the Sunni Islamic belief in predestination, or divine preordainment it has been accepted that God has full knowledge and control over all that occurs. This is explained in Qur'anic verses such as 'Say: 'Nothing will happen to us except what Allah has decreed for us: He is our protector…' For Muslims, everything in the world that occurs, good or evil, has been preordained and nothing can happen unless permitted by God. According to Muslim theologians, although events are pre-ordained, man possesses free will in that he has the faculty to choose between right and wrong, and is thus responsible for his actions.

The Shi'a understanding of free will is called 'divine justice' (*Adalah*). This doctrine, originally developed by the Mu'tazila' stresses the importance of man's responsibility for his own actions. In contrast, the Sunni de-emphasise the role of individual free will in the context of God's creation and foreknowledge of all things.

Five Pillars of Islam

These are also considered as duties in Islam. These are:

1. ***Shahadah*** (I testify that there is none worthy of worship except God and I testify that Muhammad is the Messenger of God.) It is the basic tenet of Islam. It must be recited under an oath with the following specific statement:

2. ***Salah*** (Namaz/Prayer) must be performed five times each day by keeping certain priorities, expressing gratitude and a personal communication with Him. The prayers are recited in Arabic and consist of verses from the *Qur'an*.
3. ***Sawm,*** (fasting in the month of Ramadan). Muslims must not eat or drink (among other things) from dawn to dusk during this month, and must be mindful of other sins. The fast is to encourage a feeling of gratitude to God, and during it Muslims should express their gratitude for and dependence on him, seek forgiveness for their past sins, and think of the needy.
4. ***Zakat*** (A fixed portion is spent to help the poor or needy, and also to assist the spread of Islam). The alms-giving is the practice to give based on accumulative wealth, and is obligatory for all Muslims who can afford it. The *zakat* is considered a religious obligation (as opposed to voluntary charity).
5. **Hajj** (It is the pilgrimage during the Islamic month of Dhu al-Hijjah in the city of Mecca). Every able bodied Muslim who can afford, must make the pilgrimage to Mecca at least once in his or her lifetime. The pilgrim is honoured in his or her community, although Islamic teachers say that the Hajj should be an expression of devotion to God instead of a means to gain social standing.

Etiquette and diet

Many practices fall in the category of ***adab***, or Islamic etiquette. This includes greeting others with 'as-salamu alaykum' (peace be unto you), saying ***bismillah*** (***in the name of God***) before meals, and starting any good wank and using only the right hand for eating and drinking. Islamic hygienic practices mainly fall into the category of personal cleanliness and health. Muslims are restricted in their diet and certain kind of food is prohibited to be eaten by a Muslim during all the occasions.

Sufism in Islam

Islamic law was advanced greatly by the efforts of the early 9th century jurist Al-Shafi'i who codified a method to establish the reliability of *Hadith.* Some philosophers sought to incorporate Greek principles into Islamic theology, while some others (in the 11th century) argued against them and ultimately prevailed. Finally, Sufism and Shi'ism both underwent major changes. Sufism became a full-fledged movement that had moved towards mysticism and away from its ascetic roots, while Shi'ism split due to disagreements over the succession of Imams. In the meantime some devout Muslims began to question the piety of indulgence in a worldly life, emphasizing, rather, poverty, humility, and avoidance of sin based on renunciation of bodily desires. Devout Muslim ascetic exemplars such as Hasan al-Basri inspired a movement that would evolve into Sufism.

Not strictly a denomination, Sufism is a mystical-ascetic form of Islam. By focusing on the more spiritual aspects of religion, Sufis strive to obtain direct experience of God by making use of intuitive and emotional faculties that one must be trained to use. Sufism and Islamic law are usually considered to be complementary, although Sufism has been criticized by some Muslims for being unjustified religious innovations.

Impact on Education

It is not necessary that a movement in history, philosophy or religion must affect the life and ways of people only when their ideologies are taught formally in a classroom. It is also not necessary that all education could be a formal experience. People are educated in so many ways that include exposure to a new situation, impelling by some internal feelings to learn and to change, impact of religion and others. In view of this, the influence of Islam has been very great on its people as it leads them to accept the best things in life. It includes total belief in God without any questioning, formal prayers and practising the five pillars of Islam. The impact of these is colossal on any individual who follows Islam. I reckon, there cannot be a better way of educating people than the Islamic ideology which always helps improving ways of life leading to high moral standard. Some basic features that need to be highlighted under Islamic educational excellence are:

1. According to Muslim theologians, although events are pre-ordained, man possesses free will in that he has the faculty to choose between right and wrong, and is thus responsible for his actions. The Shi'a understanding of free will is called 'divine justice' (*Adalah*). This doctrine, originally developed by the Mu'tazila' stresses the importance of man's responsibility for his own actions.

2. Many practices fall in the category of Islamic etiquette. This includes greeting others with '*as-salamu alaykum*', saying *bismillah* before meals, and using only the right hand for eating and drinking. Islamic hygienic practices mainly fall into the category of personal cleanliness and health. Muslims

are restricted in their diet and certain kind of food is prohibited to be eaten by a Muslim during all the occasions.

3. Five Pillars of Islam include Shahadah (profession of Faith), Salat (prayer), Zakat (giving alms), Sawm (fasting during Ramadan) and Hajj (pilgrimage to Mecca). These pillars always help an individual to keep him/her in awareness of the necessary duties in life for his/her own self and for the others as well.

4. Above all it is the unconditional belief in God. This is certainly going to help an individual in many ways, such as to keep away from un-virtuous activities, and to extend help to his/her own people, though it is considered paramount in other religions too.

Questions

1. How does Islam educate its followers? What are its main aspects that exert constant influence on individuals and go on educating them?

2. How do Islamic tenets influence an individual as far as their day to day life and conduct are concerned? Discuss briefly.

3. Does Sufism differ from the basic principles of Islamic religion? If not, then discuss its common aspects with that of Islam briefly.

4. Compare the Idealistic approach of 'free will' with that of Islamic concept of 'free will' as against 'predestination'. Comment critically.

REFERENCES

1. Plato : (1888) : *Republic* : Oxford: Tr by Benjamin Jowett
2. Rose, James : (1971) : *Ground Work of Educational Theory* : London : George G. Harrap & Co. Ltd.
3. Verma, I. B. : (1969) : *Basic Education* : Agra : Sri Ram Mehra
4. Brubacher, J. S. : (1950) : *Modern Philosophies of Education* : New York : McGraw Hill
5. Dewey, John : (1953) : *Democracy and Education* : New York : Macmillan
6. Mill, J. S. : (1931) : *On Education* : Cambridge : Cambridge University Press.
7. Sharma, A. P. and Hyland, J. T. : (1982) : *Philosophy of Education for Nigeria* : Jaipur : Vikas Publications, India
8. Thakur, A.S. : (1977) : *The Philosophical Foundation of Education* : New Delhi : National Publishing House
9. Dewey, John : (1916) : *Democracy and Education* : New York : The Macmillan
10. Wilson, William and Sugarman : *Introduction to moral Education* : London
11. Fontana, D. : (1981) : *Psychology for Teachers* : London :

Macmillan

12. Dewey, J. : (1976) : *Education and Experience* : London : Collier Books
13. UNESCO : (1966) : *The World Year Book of Education: Church and State Education* : Paris
14. Adams J. : (1922) : *Modern Developments in Educational Practice* : London : University of London Press
15. Montessori M. : (1912) : *The Montessori Method* : London : Heinemann
16. Rousseau J. J. : (1762) : *Emile* : London : Everyman Ed. J. M. Dent & Sons Ltd., 1966
17. Hoernle R. F. : (1924) : *Idealism as a Philosophical Doctrine* : (London : Hodder & Stoughton
18. Horne H. H. : (1932) : *The Democratic Theory of Education* : New York : Macmillan
19. Brubacher J. S. : (1969) : *Modern Philosophies of Education* : New York : McGraw Hill Book C
20. Kant I. : (1966) : *Critique of Pure Reason* : New York : Anchor Books
21. Rusk R. R. : (1956) : *The Philosophical Bases of Education* : London : University of London press
22. James W. : (1943) : *Pragmatism. A New Name for Same Old Ways of Thinking*: London : Longman
23. Harper R. : (1955) : *Modern Philosophies of Education and the Philosophic Mind* : London G. Harrap
24. Sartre J. P. : (1956) : *Existentialism is a Humanism* ; in

Kaufmann W. (Ed) : *From Dostoevsky to Sartre* : New York, Cleveland : Meridian

25. Ranade, R.D. Constructive Survey of Upanisadic Philosophy
26. Sharma A.P., O.P. Sharma, D.P. Singh (1999) Shiksha Darshan; Jaipur: Rajasthan Prakashan. India.
27. Sharma R.N. (1972) Indian Philosophy; Orient Longman Ltd.
28. Bhasker Mishra (2008) Shiksha Darshan; Delhi: Nag Publishers.
29. Rabindranath Tagore , Wikipedia, the free encyclopedia
30. Catherine Bush, (1985) World Leaders Past & Present: GANDHI; New York: Chelesa House Publishers.
31. Swami Vivekananda, Wikipedia, the Free Encyclopedia
32. Islam, Wikipedia, the Free Encyclopedia.
33. Concept of Freedom :J. Krishnamurti
34. Sharma A. P., New York: I Universe, 2000

